THE REFERENCE SHELF   VOLUME 33 NUMBER 2

BRITAIN
IN THE SIXTIES

EDITED BY ROBERT THEOBALD

THE H. W. WILSON COMPANY

NEW YORK   1961

THE REFERENCE SHELF

The books in this series reprint articles, excerpts from books, and addresses on current issues, social trends, and other aspects of American life, and occasional surveys of foreign countries. There are six separately bound numbers in each volume, all of which are generally published in the same calendar year. One number is a collection of recent speeches on a variety of subjects; each of the remaining numbers is devoted to a single subject and gives background information and discussion from varying points of view, followed by a comprehensive bibliography.

Subscribers to the current volume receive the books as issued. The subscription rate is $10 ($12 foreign) for a volume of six numbers. The price of single numbers is $2.50 each.

Copyright © 1961
By The H. W. Wilson Company
Library of Congress Catalog Card No. 61-6702

PRINTED IN THE UNITED STATES OF AMERICA

PREFACE

All the countries of the world have had to react and adjust to basically new conditions in the years since the end of the Second World War. In Britain, these forces, although perhaps less obvious there than in other areas of the world, have led to what can be adequately described only as revolutionary changes. The object of this volume is to try to show what these forces have been, to document their effects, and to give the reader the material which will permit him to perceive the outline of the choices facing Britain at the beginning of the 1960's.

Economic constraints have been of major importance in determining the course Britain has been able to follow in these years. During the Second World War Britain very largely exhausted her international credit, and at its end even owed large sums to many countries in the Commonwealth and elsewhere. Internally, goods had been in extremely scarce supply for a period of more than five years, and large sums had been accumulated in savings. Britain was therefore faced with a need to export more goods than ever before at a time when the population both wanted and felt entitled to a higher standard of living to compensate for the privations of the war years.

The imbalance between the amount of goods which people wanted to buy and the quantity actually available for purchase was further increased by the payment of large discharge gratuities to those who had served in the armed forces and also by many of the measures taken by the Labour government which came into power even before the end of the war against Japan. Repeatedly during the six years the Labour party was in power, serious crises in the field of foreign exchange occurred, and on more than one occasion Britain would have been unable to meet her international obligations without United States help.

For Britain, as for the other European powers, the American Marshall Plan was the major factor which enabled it to overcome the worst of the postwar shortages. When the Conservative government came to power in 1951, it found a greatly improved situation and was therefore able steadily to abolish the rationing of food which had continued throughout the six years of Labour party rule. The Conservatives' advantage in coming to power at a time when economic forces were working in their favor largely accounts for their success in gaining a second and then a third period in power—the latter with an unprecedented increase in their parliamentary majority.

Old and new forces have worked together during these postwar years to produce a new fabric of society whose texture is still changing and is little understood. The first section of this book examines some of the forces at work in Britain in postwar years. The second section examines the results of the pressures from these forces—the new form of society developing in Britain, which appears to bear more than a passing resemblance to that perceived in the United States by many observers.

Despite the success of the Conservative party in retaining power through the changes that have taken place in the last decade, many of those concerned with the long-range future of Britain are deeply disturbed by the party's failure to solve certain international problems or to grasp what they consider to be the realities of the new world in which we live. For many the Suez episode—the British and French invasion of Egypt following nationalization of the Suez Canal, which was subsequently condemned not only by the United States but also by most members of the Commonwealth—symbolized the failure of the Conservative party in this field.

The international issues were brought to a head in the question of Britain's relation to the Commonwealth and Europe, a conflict which has not yet been resolved. A relatively small, but growing, number of people feel that Britain must reduce though not abandon her Commonwealth role in order to form part of the "European" movement which will clearly result in the appearance of a single major power on the Continent within a limited —if uncertain—period of years. Such a policy is opposed by many, including the traditionalists, who argue that it would mean the abandonment of all Britain's worth-while goals. The arguments on both sides of this question are set out in Section III.

Britain's choice has certainly been made more difficult by the fact, which she has had to accept, that she can no longer be one of the major powers—that only two countries can aspire to this position in a nuclear age. In addition, she has also had to adjust her policy to the fact that if a nuclear war should break out, no conceivable defense policy could prevent her territory from being finally and utterly devastated. The implications of these facts have still not been completely understood, but they have already led to a neutralist movement whose strength is probably not yet fully developed. In this area Britain's problems are the same as those of many other European powers: the decisions each of them makes will be one of the crucial factors determining America's policies in the coming decades. This range of issues is discussed in the last section of the book.

The editor wishes to thank the various authors, publishers and organizations that have granted permission for the use of materials included in this book. Without their cooperation he could not have completed the volume.

ROBERT THEOBALD

March 1961

CONTENTS

PREFACE 3

I. THE THREADS OF PAST AND PRESENT

Editor's Introduction 9
Morris, James. The Timeless Flow of Ritual ....
.... New York Times Magazine 10
Hinton, R. W. K. The Prime Minister as an Elected
    Monarch .... Listener 15
Education in Britain 22
The "11 Plus" and GCE Examinations .... British Affairs 27
Cook, Don. Socialized Medicine ..... Harper's Magazine 32
Youths Leave Britain .... U.S. News & World Report 43

II. THE CONTEMPORARY FABRIC

Editor's Introduction 47
Politics in Great Britain .... Time 49
Middleton, Drew. The British Tory—Far from Tory ....
.... New York Times Magazine 55
Marquand, David. England's Labour Party . . Commentary 59
The Economy 70
Waggoner, W. H. Slow Economic Progress ....
.... New York Times 73
Nuclear Energy in Britain 75
Town Planning in London .... Atlantic Monthly 79
Crawley, Aidan. The Affluent Society in Britain ....
.... Sunday Times 83
Sampson, Anthony. Are the English Being Americanized?
.... Saturday Review 90

MacKenzie, Norman. England and Her Race Problem ...
.... Harper's Magazine 94
Titmuss, Richard M. The Irresponsible Society ... Listener 104

III. BRITAIN, EUROPE, AND THE COMMONWEALTH

Editor's Introduction 111
Cook, Don. Britain and Europe at Sixes and Sevens .....
.... Reporter 112
Lloyd, Selwyn. The British Position 118
The Structure and Meaning of the Commonwealth ....
.... British Affairs 123
Will the British Commonwealth Hold Together? ....
.... U.S. News & World Report 128
Macmillan, Harold. Commonwealth Independence and In-
terdependence .... Vital Speeches of the Day 132
Britain Faces a Major Shift ... U.S. News & World Report 138

IV. NUCLEAR POWER AND THE EAST-WEST CONFLICT

Editor's Introduction 142
Birnbaum, Norman. The Campaign for Nuclear Disarma-
ment .... Nation 142
Middleton, Drew. The Deeper Meaning of British Neutral-
ism .... New York Times Magazine 146
Calder, Ritchie. The Non-Nuclear Club ....
.... Bulletin of the Atomic Scientists 153
Middleton, Drew. British Still Hope for Summit ....
.... New York Times 157
Roosevelt, Eleanor; Russell, Bertrand; Gaitskell, Hugh;
Lord Boothby; and McKenzie, Robert. Prospects of
Mankind .... Listener 161

BIBLIOGRAPHY 179

I. THE THREADS OF PAST AND PRESENT

EDITOR'S INTRODUCTION

Many factors have contributed to the changes in the way of life in Britain in the years since the war. Some of them go far back into history, although the direction of their influence has often changed greatly in the twentieth century. The first two articles in Section I deal with the more pervasive institutions: the importance of ritual in British life and the extraordinarily powerful position of the Prime Minister in England today. The articles which follow are concerned with postwar trends.

Recent developments in the British educational system, which differs from that of the United States, have provoked much discussion. The third article in this section gives a general overview of the British educational structure. The following selection, "The '11 plus' and GCE examinations," looks at an approach which has led to the criticism, both in England and abroad, that the whole future of the child can be seriously damaged by a failure in a single examination.

Another basic change in the years since the war has been the "socialization" of much of the economy. Despite the polemic on the subject, many experts would argue that British Railways, despite its nationalized status, has as much freedom of action as the heavily regulated railroads in the United States, or even more. The program which has aroused perhaps the most attention in the United States, however, has been the British Health Service. In the article "Socialized Medicine, Ten Years Old," Don Cook shows that there are now no real opponents to free health care, and that critics of "security from the cradle to the grave" argue from a different standpoint. The concluding article points out that a significant portion of the young people think they are unable to find the opportunities they deserve and are therefore considering emigration.

THE TIMELESS FLOW OF RITUAL [1]

A clatter of hoofs, a flutter of pennants, the glint of a breast-plate and the wave of a plume, the slow swaying of a gilded coach, a tall, black line of bearskins, heralds, old men in gold cloth and wigs, a timeless, slow, measured, impeccable flow of ritual: the English, with their habitual pageantry, once again the other day opened a session of Parliament.

No other nation on earth celebrates its state events with such flamboyance, all the more dazzling to experience against the gray, muted, often shabby ambiance of London in November. Few other peoples in the world still inject into their daily lives such insidious doses of ceremony and parade. It is not that the English are showy by nature. . . . Their manners are usually un-ceremonious, even by American standards, and they shudder at a florid compliment or an ornate good-by. Their very idiom is generally terse and condensed and their humor relies more than most on the dry, the rapier thrust and the ironic. The English are not half so reserved as they are popularly supposed to be, just as their London fogs do not occur, as Hollywood would have us suppose, every Friday evening, but neither are they, in their personal customs, a people of elaborate or decorative tastes.

Yet through their affairs there runs, as every travel agent knows, a constant stubborn streak of glitter, display and ostenta-tion—even now, with their Empire gone and their proud fleets dispersed and their rate of production, so the economists gloom-ily reiterate, lazily lagging behind that of their rivals. . . .

At the pinnacle of their hierarchy is the Queen—surrounded by a gilded screen of ceremony. From time to time, dauntless reformers try to demolish it, protesting as they do so that nobody is more essentially royalist than they. But the national judgment seems to be that a democratic, workaday Queen—a Queen with-out mystery—would be worse than no Queen at all. Queen Elizabeth thus moves in a miasma of ritual, so that even at the most prosaic of chores—the inspection of a pig-iron factory or

[1] From "Again the Timeless Flow of Ritual," by James Morris, author and correspondent for the Manchester *Guardian*. New York *Times Magazine*. p 38-9+. N. 13, '60. Reprinted by permission.

a garden party of the Society for the Abolition of Sin—she seems
to be attended by the shadows of chamberlains and the gleam
of cuirasses.

Her coronation in 1953 was, I suppose, the most glittering
pageant of our era, far outshining in exotic splendor any remnants of oriental extravagance. Her royal palaces are guarded
with endless permutations of parade. When she goes on a state
procession, the jingling troopers of her Household Cavalry, like
figures from the heroic past, escort her coach in resplendent
phalanx.

Even when she takes a train to Scotland the stationmaster
stands on the platform in a top hat, indescribably respectful,
archaic and feudal against the dim, grimy purlieus of Euston
Station. One of the poignant moments of contemporary historical experience is to wander down the Duke of York's Steps in
high summer to stand on tiptoe beneath the plane trees of the
Mall and peer over the heads of the crowds and the high-helmet-
ed policemen to catch a glimpse of the Queen of the English at
the head of her Household troops. In scarlet jacket and tricorne
hat, seated sidesaddle on a chestnut, she rides down toward the
Admiralty Arch in that gala among ceremonies, trooping the
colors. No spectacle of our time reeks of history so or is richer
in glamour, romance, mystery—and swank. . . .

The pulse of circumstance also beats—sometimes incongru-
ously and sometimes absurdly—through the professional strata
of English life, far removed from the guns and the bugle calls.
The old universities of Oxford and Cambridge are shot through
with strands of ceremony—from the dons solemnly circulating
the port in the Common Room to all the paraphernalia of maces,
scrolls and embroidered fineries accompanying the installation of
a chancellor, or the award of an honorary degree.

The pomp of medieval origins sometimes brings a comic
consequence to the assemblies of the City Guilds. The Worshipful Companies of Skinners, Curriers, Painters, Turners and
Carpenters roll into their high-vaulted halls with all the glittering complacency of merchant princes. I once looked up in the
course of a newsreel to see some such London ceremonial unroll-

ing its events upon the screen and there in the very foreground
of the picture, advancing toward me with awful and stately gait,
was an old acquaintance of mine, normally to be seen in modest
tweeds and a self-effacing tie, reading a detective story in the
club library.

He was dressed from head to foot in cloth of gold. He
carried a silver wand in his hands. On his head, there was a
queer tricorne cap, and he looked for all the world like a cross
between an oriental satrap and an unusually ornate playing card.
It is an odd feeling, thus to see the conceptions of a lifetime
shattered. . . .

So down the English order the appetite for pomp is satisfied,
from Queen to Lord Great Chamberlain, from Chief of the
Imperial General Staff to Deputy Warden of the Worshipful
Company of Fishmongers, from the Senior Proctor, with his
bulldogs at Oxford, to His Worship, the Mayor of Little Bug-
gleston. He is perhaps the grandest of them all, with his red
robes and his chain of office and his air of unassailable authority,
standing like a prophet or a patriarch on the gallery of his town
hall on Guy Fawkes Night.

Of course, there are wide segments of English life no more
enmeshed in pageantry than are, say, the Jersey City waterworks.
Few men in England, though, stand beyond the appeal of gilded
tradition, and no woman at all, I venture to suggest, is altogether
impervious to the call of majesty, grandeur or royalty—or horo-
scopes, for that matter. There is an element of superstition to
this addiction, and an element of something approaching ani-
mism. The phenomenon of royalty in England, with its extraordinary hold on the imaginations of ordinary people, bears a
distinct resemblance to some of the nobler West African fetish
cults.

More to the point, there is also a potent element of insular
independence. The prime exponents of pageantry in the world
are the British, the Japanese and the Venetians, islanders all.
They are all people cut off by water from the hinterland and
they have, therefore, cherished astonishingly strong mores of
their own—strong enough to have survived that shrinking of the

world, that fusion of cultures, that has come with the age of the radio and the aircraft.

Kyoto, with its private treasures and its myriad festivals, bears a strong spiritual resemblance to an English city, for all its absolute physical disparity. Generations of observers have noticed how closely the affairs of the Venetians and the English have run parallel—the same aristocratic society, the same protectivism, the same emphasis on color, display and all the trappings of power. Islanders are not necessarily individualists, but they tend to be a prickly kind of people. Beneath their crusty shells of reserve or secrecy you often find, like pearls in a horny oyster, the glitter of proud self-sufficiency coupled, as often as not, with a trace of inbreeding that makes for wrinkled devices and eccentricities.

For several centuries, many of the traditions of the English have remained inviolate and honored, until they are ingrained in the very fabric of the place, like gold dust lodged in the crevices of a rock. The very existence of Britain, the outrider of Europe, is a pageant in itself. The parade of England begins at the white cliffs of Dover which stand there on a sunlit day high, white and awfully noble, like a line of tall sentinels above the sea. "Liquid history" is how an old radical once described the river Thames, and, by the same token, those Shakespearean ramparts are pedigrees of chalk.

Like the Venetians, the English have fostered their pageantry as a matter of state policy. In times of hardship it has often served them well. Bags of swank undoubtedly helped to win the war and in the bleak years afterward, when the Empire was disintegrating, when the currency was devalued, when food was scarce and nylons were scarcer, when every football game seemed doomed to defeat and every tennis champion was American, when around the world British policy was reviled, rebuffed or riddled with doubt—in those drab days, the color and splendor of English ceremonial, shrewdly maintained despite it all, provided a changeless core of certainty.

Whatever has happened to India, the Olympic team or the pound sterling (so ran the subconscious reasoning of the English), at least the monarchy is all ours, and nobody at all—not the bloody Yanks or old Joe Stalin himself—can march down to Buckingham Palace quite like a company of grenadiers. . . .

In maintaining . . . evenness and steadiness of behavior, the glamour of pageantry has played its paradoxical part. A nation can be anesthetized by too much tradition or too Ruritanian a sense of parade. The Venetians succumbed to it in the end. Sometimes the English stagger, too, when too strong a whiff of it blows down Whitehall. ("Wake Up, Fairyland," was the salutary headline in one of the Chicago newspapers a couple of mornings after Coronation Day.) The beat of the drums and the flaunt of the standards can also be, though, if they are kept free of arrogance and chauvinism, valuable safety valves for national emotions.

The English will never be militarists so long as they prefer a brave toy soldier in a sentry box to the toughest young thug with a burp gun, so long as they care more about the scrapping of some beloved but long obsolete battleship than they do about the prestige of nuclear potential. You have only to compare the hideous manifestations of Hitler's way—the mammoth shouting parades, the crooked banners and the cruel poses—to understand how mellowing an influence has been the millennium of British tradition, how happily a sense of occasion can go with a sense of humor.

For do not suppose that the English take all their ritual solemnly. Much of it is done frankly for fun and much of it strikes everybody, even the participants, as being distinctly touched with lunacy.

So there they go through London, as they have down the generations—the lance pennants fluttering, the accoutrements jangling, the old coach creaking and wobbling and bouncing about, the cavalrymen ruddy but stern-faced as sphinxes, the coachmen periwigged, the outriders swinging along with drawn swords gleaming, the crowds self-consciously cheering, the foot soldiers statuesque, the bobbies as stolid as time itself. And, down the road at Westminster, wait the Parliamentarians, the Peers and the Commons, Her Majesty's Government and Her

Majesty's Loyal Opposition—from the loftiest earl to the cockiest Welsh miner, from the true-bluest of Tories to the pinkest of fellow-traveling-ban-the-bomb Socialists.

Scarcely a soul down there, I suspect, however irrepressible his instincts of protest and progress, would abolish one gesture, one medal, one ribbon, one silk glove, one small flourish of this ancient splendor. For it is more than an obsolete ritual based on the kingships of long ago. It is consistency and it is inconsequence. It is pride and it is pathos. It is loyalty and purpose, and it is frivolity, too. It is policy. It is nonsense. It is extravagance. It is cheap at the price. It is history. It is art. It is England, our England.

THE PRIME MINISTER AS AN ELECTED MONARCH [2]

When I suggest that the best name for . . . [the British] constitution is "elective monarchy" it is not out of a secret wish to change the constitution. I think our constitution is a very good one and only wish to describe it more accurately. Words do matter. They are the tools with which we manipulate ideas, and political ideas require to be handled accurately. While new countries with fully fledged constitutions spring up all round us, many of them modeled more or less closely on ours, our constitution deserves the most exact definition we can give it. [The author uses the term "constitution" to mean form of government. Britain does not have a written constitution.—Ed.] Democracy is not a very useful word as we use it nowadays. "Democratic" seems to mean anything from "egalitarian," which is what it means when we speak of a democratic society, to "just," which is what it means when people sometimes speak of an action being democratic. Often it is simply a synonym for "free," so that the world is sometimes said to be divided into democracies and dictatorships, as if these were the only two kinds of political organization.

[2] Reprint of British Broadcasting Company talk by R. W. K. Hinton, Fellow of Peterhouse and lecturer in history at the University of Cambridge. *Listener.* 113:158-9. Ja. 28, '60. Reprinted by permission.

Words are useful when they enable us to make distinctions, but this woolly terminology prevents them and is one of the reasons why political thought is at a low ebb nowadays. For example, there are important differences between the French, American, and British constitutions, and to call them all democracies is to obscure their distinguishing characteristics. Moreover, democracy is an old term: but for more than two thousand years it was a term for a bad kind of constitution; only in the last hundred years has it become a term of praise. This reversal of meaning has made all the good old political thought, from Plato to the eighteenth century, look in some way remote and defective, as if the old thinkers, clever as they were, were somehow missing the one obvious important truth: so that you find schoolboys making excuses for Plato and Aristotle; while the modern debate on contemporary political problems suffers from undernourishment because it cannot draw on the rich debates of the past.

But perhaps our constitution is not a democracy. If democracy means anything exact it means government by the people. All government is *of* the people, and all good government is *for* the people, but only democratic government is *by* the people. In Britain the people may be sovereign but they do not govern. They elect a Prime Minister to govern for them. Government by a single person is monarchy, and it is because the Prime Minister is the real ruler that I think our constitution ought to be called a monarchy. We recognize this in practice when we vote. We vote for a man who is to be Prime Minister or for a set of ideas with which he is associated. It is possible to vote effectively—and many people do—without knowing anything about the local candidate except his name; his personality and ideas are not important. It is the ideas and personalities of the men who are candidates for the position of Prime Minister which are important. And when we have elected a Prime Minister that man rules until the next general election.

For look next at the Prime Minister's power. Since a Prime Minister without a majority in the House of Commons is an impossibility, he is in a position to make any law he thinks fit.

The House of Lords cannot stand against the House of Commons; the Queen's consent is, as far as one can see, automatic; and the constitution puts no limit to what a parliamentary law can do. Without a written constitution and without even a constitution which is held to be fixed, any law made in Parliament is absolutely binding. No court of law would dream of resisting an act of Parliament. There is not even in this country any considerable body of opinion which holds that an act of Parliament would be invalid if it conflicted with the law of nature or the law of God: our political thinking has no place nowadays for higher laws than acts of Parliament. So the parliamentary power of the Prime Minister with his automatic majority in the House of Commons is completely irresistible. It is in fact an arbitrary power; a power which in former days in the hands of hereditary kings might well have been called tyrannical.

Diplomacy Outside Parliament

But the Prime Minister's parliamentary power is not all his power. He has also a large measure of power which is not parliamentary, the power of the prerogative, a power all the greater because ill defined. The Prime Minister does not require a parliamentary majority to declare war, and all his diplomacy is done outside Parliament. There is also the domestic prerogative which we generally see being exercised by the Home Secretary. The Home Secretary acts under the prerogative when he pardons criminals. He can also rest on the prerogative when there is a question of public security. There was an example of this a few years ago when the Home Secretary was questioned in the House of Commons concerning the tapping of private telephone conversations. Some members demanded a full explanation, but the Home Secretary said: "No, sir, I am not prepared to go into detail in this matter, which derives from the prerogative and which is a power that I should exercise at my discretion." Members did not like that answer, but the Home Secretary stuck to it. "Any government," he said, "must take precautions to secure public order and the security of the state.

There is no question of there being any enlargement of powers which are an acknowledged part of any government and which do not form a very suitable subject for public debate.''

The Prime Minister is really two persons in one, a king as well as the leader of the major party in the House of Commons. Our constitution says that he is the Queen's servant, her chief minister, but it also says that the Queen is bound to accept his advice. He has inherited the prerogative power from a long line of kings who for centuries jealously guarded it and often exercised it, and he has joined to it the parliamentary power which the Houses of Parliament asserted for five or six centuries against the King's prerogative. The prerogative and the parliamentary powers taken together give the Prime Minister at least as much power as any other ruler of the present day and probably more than any English ruler of the past.

This does not mean that the Prime Minister's power is unlimited, but there are no constitutional limits to his power, only prudential ones of the sort which all wise rulers are careful to observe. What our constitution does is to persuade the Prime Minister to be wise, because if he behaves in practice as arbitrarily as he can in theory, he ceases to be Prime Minister.

Last Word in the Cabinet

Yet even in practice he has a good deal of freedom. The constitution gives him a Cabinet, and it is undoubtedly convenient for him to carry the Cabinet with him in his decisions. Yet the ministers who form the Cabinet are appointed by him in the same way as the king's council in former days was appointed by the king. Every monarch must take advice, prime ministers no less than kings. But there is no doubt that the Prime Minister has the last word in the Cabinet just as kings had the last word in the council. Again, the Prime Minister must not provoke a rebellion among his followers in the House of Commons. That is a real restraint but a more remote one than we perhaps like to imagine. For a revolt of the Prime Minister's own party would not put the rebels in power but the opposition, and a Prime Minister would have to act very provocatively before his party would be willing to do that.

Again, the Prime Minister wishes to be reelected at the next election and therefore he must avoid antagonizing the people at large; but this, too, is a less severe restraint than one might think. He has come to power with a wide and generally imprecise mandate. It is unavoidable in a two-party system that each candidate for the position of Prime Minister will stand for a general set of ideas rather than a few exact ones. Therefore if a Prime Minister does one thing which his electors do not like, this does not mean that they will elect next time a rival candidate who is likely to do three or four things which they will not like. In any case the need to keep the people in a good temper is more likely to operate negatively in preventing the Prime Minister from doing something which he would like to do than in positively compelling him to do something which he does not want to do. Since all rulers depend ultimately on the consent of the people, whatever their theoretical powers, these limitations are little more of a restraint than those which limited the power of hereditary monarchs in past times.

Above all one must remember that to oust one Prime Minister is merely to put in another. The constitution does not allow the people to change the powers of the Prime Minister but only the person who exercises them. No Prime Minister is likely to desire less power than his predecessor and, therefore, five-yearly changes of government do not make the Prime Minister any less of a monarch.

Democracy—a Rare Form of Government

Democracy is a much rarer form of government than is often supposed. Democracy is possible in a pure form only in small societies where all the members can meet, and where they all agree as to the end in view, understand the difficulties, and have an equal knowledge as to how to overcome them. Thus in a tennis club all the members can meet with a common aim and a common understanding of the situation, and can vote for a course of action binding on all. That is pure democracy: the people are governing themselves. In large states of millions of people who cannot meet, who have no clearly defined common object, and who cannot equally understand their problems, democracy has to operate indirectly through elected assemblies. The signs of democracy in large states with elected assemblies are frequent elections, a multiparty system, exact mandates, plural voting, and governments which are party coalitions forming and reforming according to the particular object aimed at at any moment. If such a government wishes to impose a tax, it may have to win the support of a group of representatives who have been elected on a no-tax platform. If it has ideas about educational reform, it may have to take account of the representatives who have been elected with specific instructions concerning education. To win the support of one party for one purpose it may well find itself bound to accede to that party's demands for another purpose, and its policy will, therefore, follow fairly closely demands which the people themselves have formulated. In such a state it may be said that the people govern themselves, and therefore the constitution may be called a democracy. That was the French system until the late constitutional revolution—obviously entirely different from the British system. To lump together that system and the British system under the name of democracy is, therefore, to obscure what most British people probably regard as the merits of the British system.

Sometimes the British system is called constitutional or limited monarchy, but those terms are unrealistic. We have not had limited monarchy since the days of Queen Victoria or earlier. Monarchy and royalty are totally different things. Monarchy is a term of political analysis meaning government by a single person. Royalty refers to status and is a matter of inheritance and blood. The Queen is royal but she does not govern and therefore she cannot properly be called a monarch. At the present day the greatest constitutional or limited monarchy would appear to be the Federal Government of the United States. The American President's position is correctly likened to that of the

English King in the time of William III. William III had great powers: he was the head of the executive branch of government, he was head of the armed forces; he appointed whom he liked to serve him and he took advice from whom he liked. He was limited because after 1688 the House of Commons and the House of Lords also had great powers, and although he was responsible for governing the country he could not govern it in opposition to the wishes of the Houses of Parliament. That seems to be the President's position in the Federal Constitution of the United States. Its characteristic is that the supreme political power is shared between a single man and the elected representatives of the people. But we have changed all that. The British Prime Minister combines the powers of the single man and of the elected assembly, and that is why I see nothing for it but to call him a monarch.

The Queen's Greatest Glory

This does not mean that the Queen's part in our constitution is unimportant. It is very important. Queen Elizabeth I said that she accounted it the greatest glory of her reign to have ruled with her people's love. Queen Elizabeth II will say the same. Rulers who value the people's love are more likely to rule sincerely and well than those who simply value their votes. One of the virtues without which our system would be insupportable is that the Prime Minister in some sort shares in this regal sentiment when he takes over the regal power. In past times when people discussed the advantages and disadvantages of hereditary monarchy they found that one of the advantages was that a hereditary ruler was not swayed from moment to moment by gusts of popular opinion, but could govern sternly and look to the future. The hereditary king was supposed to be able to recognize, however dimly and fallibly, the general long-term interest of the whole people; he did not have to govern in the interests of particular sections of the people or even in the interest of a single generation. It was not a bad argument. Rulers who govern in that spirit probably do govern better than those who are led to think too much about the next general election. British Prime Ministers should seek votes, yet the tradition that they are the Queen's servant is a powerful though intangible influence.

I hope it will not be thought ridiculous to say that the people still accept that tradition, even if they do not recognize it for what it is; and that they expect the Prime Minister to rise on occasion above the demands of vote catching and to act more responsibly, more conscientiously, and with a greater regard for long-term good than if he was simply a president whose chief aim was to be reelected after five years. It is the Queen who keeps this tradition alive by imparting some of her transcendent sense of duty to the man who has taken her power, and it may well be that without a royal person it would die.

Peaceful Rebellion

It is perfectly true when all is said and done that British constitutional conventions include the idea of the sovereignty of the people. This is not incompatible with the idea of the sovereignty of the Queen, or with the idea that the Prime Minister is a monarch. It is possible to assert the sovereignty of the people even in absolute hereditary monarchies, and in fact popular sovereignty was often asserted in former times as a justification for rebellion against kings. That is exactly what the sovereignty of the people involves in Britain today—not armed rebellion but the peaceful rebellion which takes place at every general election.

EDUCATION IN BRITAIN [3]

Every boy or girl in Britain must by law attend school (or receive efficient education in some other way) from the age of 5 up to the age of 15. A small proportion of children start school at 2, 3 or 4 in a nursery school or class. About seven out of ten leave school at 15, others stay on till 16, 17, 18 or 19.

[3] From fact sheet. (Fact Sheets on Britain R 2541/8) British Information Services. 45 Rockefeller Plaza. New York 20. Ap. '58. Reprinted by permission.

The number staying beyond the minimum leaving age is increasing. The usual age of entry to the universities is 18 or 19 and the length of course for a first degree is three or four years.

Responsibility for providing school education and further education outside the universities is shared by the central department (Ministry of Education, Scottish Education Department, or Ministry of Education for Northern Ireland) and local education authorities. The universities are self-governing institutions, although nearly three quarters of their income now comes from public funds. The principal acts governing education in Britain are the Education Act, 1944 (for England and Wales), the Education (Scotland) Act, 1946, and the Education Act (Northern Ireland), 1947.

Schools

More than 90 per cent of children attend schools that are maintained by the local education authorities out of public money. Education in these schools is free. In England and Wales some of the schools maintained by local education authorities are provided by them—these are called county schools; the others, called voluntary schools, are provided by voluntary bodies, usually a church or religious denomination. County schools outnumber voluntary schools. In addition some schools (mostly grammar schools) not financed by local education authorities receive direct grants-in-aid from the Ministry of Education; they charge fees but must provide a proportion of free places.

Independent schools must be registered and are subject to official inspection. Fees are charged in these schools but, in many, some scholarships and free places are available, either from endowments or, through the local education authorities, from public funds.

The schools maintained by the local education authorities are divided into primary schools or departments for children up to 11 (12 in Scotland) and secondary schools for older boys and girls. In Scotland, boys and girls are taught together in almost all schools; in England and Wales this is usual in the primary schools but boys and girls more often than not attend separate secondary schools. Secondary schools are of different kinds: in England and Wales there are grammar schools for boys and girls who hope to go on to a university or to enter a profession, or whose abilities would fit them to do so; there are secondary modern schools for a larger proportion of children; and technical schools for a smaller number. In the technical schools, there is greater emphasis on practical and commercial subjects. Some schools provide more than one kind of secondary education and in some areas there are comprehensive schools providing all types of secondary education. Each local education authority plans its own schools, subject to the Minister's approval, and arranges how the children shall be allocated between them. In Scotland, there are two main types of secondary school, the junior secondary school providing a three-year course and the senior secondary school with five- or six-year courses.

The largest and most important of the independent schools are known in England as "public" schools, although some schools classed as public schools are not independent (most of these are direct-grant schools) and public schools form only a minority of all independent schools. The public school has made a notable contribution to English education. Many public schools date from the sixteenth century, some are older (e.g., Winchester, 1382, and Eton, 1440). All are controlled by their own boards of governors. Public schools have emphasized the importance of character building, and in these schools were developed the prefect system, whereby day-to-day discipline is largely maintained by the pupils themselves, and the house system, whereby a school is divided into groups of about fifty, each under the care of a housemaster. The public school is also characterized by a high staffing ratio and a high proportion of pupils doing advanced work. A public school is often, although not necessarily, a boarding school. The usual age of entry to the independent public schools for boys is 13 and the leaving age about 18. There are some girls' public schools modeled to a certain extent on those for boys.

There are also preparatory schools, most of them boarding schools, for boys aged from about 8 to 13 years (and some similar schools for girls) who are intending to enter public schools, and a wide range of other schools covering every age group, grade of education, and variety of educational method. Some of these schools are owned and managed, often under a trust deed, by independent non-profit-making bodies. Others are privately owned.

School Examinations

The examination for the General Certificate of Education is generally taken by grammar school pupils. A number of pupils in secondary technical schools and a small, but increasing, number of pupils in secondary modern schools take the examination. It is not restricted to pupils in England and Wales and a number of candidates take it in overseas centers. Papers are set at ordinary, advanced and scholarship levels and a certificate given for a pass in one or more subjects. Sixteen is the usual age for taking the examination at ordinary level. Further passes at higher levels or in other subjects may be added to a certificate. Appropriate passes in suitable groups of subjects satisfy the preliminary educational requirements of the universities and professional bodies. The Scottish Leaving Certificate is awarded by examination at the end of the secondary school course.

Teachers

Teachers are not employed by the central government but by the local education authority or the management of the school. They are not in general bound by official instructions as to syllabuses, textbooks or methods. There are some 150 teachers training colleges in England and Wales giving a training usually lasting two years to students aged 18 or over, and 23 university education departments providing a one-year course for graduates. The two-year course . . . [was] superseded by a three-year course in September 1960. In Scotland courses normally last one year for graduates and three years for nongraduates. In Northern Ireland also the basic course in the general training colleges lasts three years. The Education Departments, the universities, local education authorities and other bodies provide a variety of short courses for practicing teachers.

Teachers from schools in the United Kingdom go to a number of overseas countries each year under interchange schemes or schemes for temporary overseas posts.

Further Education

Increasing numbers of young workers are being released by their employers on one or two days or half days each week to take classes in trade subjects or general educational subjects. All local authorities and some other bodies provide technical colleges which offer full-time and part-time courses, some of university degree standard. Some, such as colleges of art, are specialized institutions, others are polytechnics. Fees at grant-aided establishments are moderate and many students pay no fees, for all local education authorities grant scholarships to qualified students.

Evening classes are organized by the universities, local education authorities and voluntary bodies, notably the Workers' Educational Association, and are aided by government grants. Almost any subject can be studied in these classes, whether it be academic, cultural or practical, and vocational or nonvocational. Six grant-aided residential colleges provide one-year courses for adult students, and, since the Second World War, more than twenty residential colleges have been established where adult students can take short courses lasting from a few days to a few weeks.

Technical Education

The British system of technical education is very flexible. A boy leaving school at 15, by part-time study at a technical college and practical experience in industry, can achieve professional qualifications in technology from the age of 25. Alternatively, a would-be technologist may go from school to university, or he may take a full-time course at a technical college. Technical colleges, in cooperation with industry, provide courses at craftsman level, at intermediate or technician level, as well as at advanced level. One form of advanced course is the sandwich course which lasts four or five years and involves alternate periods, usually of three to six months, of education in a technical college and training in industry. A big expansion of technical education is in progress.

THE "11 PLUS" AND GCE EXAMINATIONS [4]

A notable feature of British education is the delegation of authority and an avoidance of directives. This had led to much diversity of practice among schools, even schools in the same area. Nevertheless there are broad similarities. An important influence in bringing this about has been the public examination system. The external examinations held annually in the secondary schools and more recently the "11 plus" examinations taken by children due to transfer from the primary to secondary level have necessarily exerted a very powerful influence on the content and organization of education. They have also done much to maintain and raise standards.

"11 Plus" Examinations

One of the few statutory requirements placed upon local education authorities when planning secondary education is that it should offer "such variety of instruction and training as may be demanded in view of" their pupils' "different ages, abilities and aptitudes." This leaves local authorities free to plan secondary education in whatever form is best suited to local circumstances, but in practice most local authorities in England, Wales and Northern Ireland provide secondary education of three types, grammar (a largely academic curriculum), technical and modern (general and practical courses). In Scotland there

[4] From "Examinations!" *British Affairs*. 3:7+. Mr. '59. Reprinted by permission.

are two types of secondary education, junior for students leaving at 15 and senior for students leaving at 17 or 18.

But potential abilities and aptitudes have to be determined if they are to be developed and catered for. And it is here, at the time of transfer from the primary to secondary school that the first major educational test in the form of the "11 plus" examination must be met.

To determine the type of secondary education for which they are best suited children are tested in the spring of the school year in which they attain the age of 11. These tests are organized by the local education authorities. There is no standard practice, but the various procedures have enough features in common to make possible a description of the methods generally adopted. The form of the examination is usually such as to measure general aptitude and attainment in arithmetic and in English. . . . It should be noted that the questions are based not upon the full curriculum, since abler children will certainly have covered more ground than the questions reflect, while slow learners will not have covered as much.

The tests are administered by children's own teachers who also mark them and convert the raw scores into standardized scores so as to allow for differences in ages. The marked lists and scores are sent to the Education Office of the local authority to be checked. The order of merit list based on cumulative scores is then prepared.

The available places in grammar and in secondary technical schools determine the number of children who will be transferred to these selective schools; the remainder—on average approximately 75 per cent of the total—will go to secondary modern schools. It is accordingly possible to draw a theoretical line on the order of merit list so that the number of children above it corresponds to the selective places available. In practice it is usual to draw two lines, one above the theoretical line and another at a corresponding point below. Children whose names fall above the upper line are allocated to selective schools without further consideration. Children whose names fall between the two lines, half of whom will go to selective schools, are said to be "on the borderline." In respect of these children the examiners take into consideration additional evidence on their relative suitability for selective education. This evidence may comprise reports previously submitted by principals of primary schools, the children's school exercise books, or whatever may be gleaned from an interview; sometimes borderline children are given additional tests.

Selection at "11 plus" has been the subject of substantial criticism in the last few years. Its critics say that the tests have a harmful backwash on the work in primary schools; that young children should not be subjected to the ordeal of public examination, and that no selective process, however refined, can prognosticate subsequent successes with certainty. Public uneasiness however seems to stem mainly from the belief that a child who does not go on to a grammar school is somehow branded as inferior. In fact, of course, the vast majority go to the secondary modern school. Some education authorities are dropping the term "secondary modern" and calling these schools simply secondary or high school. But it is widely accepted that children do differ considerably in abilities and aptitudes and that these differences can be catered for, for the most part effectively, by means of grouping like with like in courses of varying difficulty. Special efforts and experiments are being made to improve the selection processes; it is likely that the practice of providing in secondary modern schools special courses leading to the General Certificate of Education examination for students whose scholastic ability develops late will be greatly accelerated. In the period 1954-57 alone the number of secondary modern students remaining at school to take the GCE examination more than doubled. A further experiment is with comprehensive secondary schools, more on the United States pattern, where the child finds his own level, whether in the scholastic stream or in technical training or again in less ambitious pursuits.

The General Certificate of Education

It has long been the practice for public examinations to be held annually in secondary schools and for the same exam system to cover state-supported and private schools alike. In England and Wales they are conducted with the approval of the Ministry of Education by examination boards set up by the universities. Similar public examinations are conducted in Scotland and Northern Ireland. In England and Wales, the recognized external examination is the General Certificate of Education (GCE). This came into being in 1951 replacing the former system of setting two examinations, known as the Higher Certificate and the School Certificate.

The new examination was established with the intention of defining the standards reached in particular subjects at a stage as late as possible in the secondary school course, primarily with a view to meeting admission requirements to a university or to courses of study in other institutions of higher education, such as technical colleges or training colleges for teachers or to professional training.

The examination papers are set at three levels: ordinary, advanced and scholarship. The ordinary papers are designed to provide a reasonable test in a subject for pupils who have taken it as part of a wide and general secondary course up to the age of at least 16. The order of popularity of subjects in the middle school can be deduced from the number of entries at ordinary level in the GCE and is as follows: English language, mathematics, English literature, French, geography, history, science, art, Latin.

For many pupils the first GCE examination marks the end of their school career, but the tendency to continue at school in order to spend a year or two in the sixth form [the highest secondary school grade] has grown steadily of recent years, and the proportion has now risen to about 40 per cent.

The advanced papers are designed to provide a reasonable test of those subjects in which students have specialized during

two or more years of sixth form study. At the advanced level
it is possible to gain a distinction mark. The age range in the
sixth form is roughly equivalent to the eleventh and twelfth
grades and the curriculum is markedly specialist in character.
It is narrowed to about five subjects of which the student will
specialize in three, devoting about two thirds of the working
week to them. Typical combinations of special subjects are
mathematics, physics and chemistry; mathematics, further mathematics and physics; English, French and Latin, English history
and Latin. The choice of subjects tends to divide the sixth form
into two sides, the science side and the arts side. It is estimated
that about 60 per cent of all sixth form students are currently
studying on the science side. This is borne out by the choice of
subjects by candidates for the GCE at the advanced level, which
is usually taken two years after sitting for the ordinary level,
the order being, physics, mathematics, chemistry, English, history,
French, biology, geography, Latin.

Scholarship papers are designed to give specially gifted students an opportunity for showing distinctive merit and promise.
The essential difference between scholarship and advanced level
lies in the nature of the questions set; they do not necessarily
cover a substantially wider field of study. Successes in the
scholarship papers provide criteria for making the awards of
state and local education authority scholarships at the universities.
At the present time 75.7 per cent of the students at British
universities receive some form of scholarship assistance.

All subjects at each level are purely optional, the candidate
taking the subjects of his choice at the level of his choice. There
are no group or minimum requirements for the Certificate, which
records the subjects and levels at which the candidate has satisfied
the examiners. However, although the universities' admission
requirements vary, it is broadly correct to say that they require
a GCE showing five or six passes of which at least two are at the
advanced level. Faculty and departmental requirements often
require advanced level in the subjects the student wishes to pursue
for his degree.

SOCIALIZED MEDICINE [5]

Ten years after the establishment of the British National Health Service it is difficult—in fact almost impossible—to find an opponent of "socialized medicine" left on this island. There are plenty of critics of the Health Service. There are doctors who are discouraged and bitter, and there are patients who complain loudly and frequently. There are individuals who would not dream of accepting free state medical treatment, and there are physicians who will have nothing to do with state-paid medical practice. But "opponents" who would turn back the clock ten years and return to the old medical system in this country are really nonexistent.

Certainly there are none among the 49,850,000 Britons (97 per cent of the population) who are registered patients of National Health Service doctors and never pay any medical bills. Among the doctors themselves, out of a total of about 49,000 in the United Kingdom, there are still a gallant 600 or so general practitioners who ride through the valley of death relying solely on fees from private patients. But even these physicians are not exactly "opponents" of socialized medicine. In fact, their practices have probably gained from improved snob appeal.

On the tenth anniversary of the establishment of the Service, the British Medical Association *Journal* was full of praise of it from leaders of the medical profession.

"From the point of view of the 'consumer' it has been an enormous benefit and success," wrote Dr. H. Guy Dain, who was chairman of the BMA Council during the crucial negotiations between doctors and the government which preceded the take-over of private practices by the state in July of 1948. "The absence of any financial barrier between doctor and patient must make the doctor-patient relationship easier and more satisfactory."

Lord Moran, personal physician to Sir Winston Churchill for many years and one of the elder statesmen of British medicine, wrote: "If consultants were asked whether they desired to go

[5] Article, "Socialized Medicine, Ten Years Old," by Don Cook, chief correspondent for the European area, and former chief of the London bureau, New York *Herald Tribune. Harper's Magazine.* 218:32-7. My. '59. Reprinted by permission.

back to the old days, I believe the overwhelming majority would prefer the conditions of today."

Iain Macleod, who was appointed Minister of Health by Sir Winston after the Conservatives came back to power, is even more sweeping and forceful about the success of socialized medicine and its soundness as political and social policy in a democracy. Now the Minister of Labour, Mr. Macleod was the son of a small-town doctor, and watched him struggle in the depression years to help poorer patients.

"I believe in the National Health Service with all my heart," he said to me. "Indeed, I believe some sort of national health service, whatever it may be called, will come in every country in the world. Not necessarily our model; it might not survive export. If we were starting again we might have based it more on insurance than we did. But other countries, including the United States, can and will benefit from our experiences, our successes, and our mistakes."

The National Health Service has, in fact, become a source of genuine national pride—like the Royal Navy or the Monarchy. Britons know that there may be more spectacular examples of medical skill or research or treatment in the United States or elsewhere. But in their country more of the population get better medical care than in any other major country on earth. Their pride is far from uncritical. But as the second decade of the Health Service begins, the emphasis is entirely on "How can we make it better?" Strikingly, the system itself, the structure, is almost universally judged to be sound.

Free Care Without Red Tape

The Service originated in the early days of this century, when the Liberals under David Lloyd George put through the first compulsory health insurance act in the country. The law was amended and expanded constantly for the next forty years, as successive Liberal, Conservative, and Labour Governments endorsed and reindorsed the principle of a state medical program.

The Labour Government of 1945-51 finally hammered out the legislation, made the basic decisions, and devised the system of free medical care for all the people as it exists in Britain today. The final architect was that dynamic left-wing Welshman, Aneurin Bevan, the Labour Minister of Health of that day. Ten years later, doctors, administrators, civil servants, and politicians of all shades of experience and opinion agree that the structure which he established was basically sound.

Perhaps the key to its soundness is its administrative simplicity so far as the patient is concerned—as I discovered in abrupt personal experience shortly after I returned to London to live three years ago. Running to catch a double-decker bus—I slipped on the pavement and came down heavily on my outstretched left arm. I was helped up in considerable pain, and realized at once that this was more serious than a bruise or sprain, although no fracture was apparent. I got into a taxi and asked to be taken to Charing Cross Hospital not far from my London office. I walked in and explained to a receptionist what had happened. She asked only four questions: name, age, address, and whether or not I was registered with a National Health Service doctor. I had no doctor in London, but that did not matter. I was not asked my nationality, or whether I had any kind of registration card, or whether I had paid any contribution to a fund, or whom I worked for, or even if I had paid my British taxes! I was simply handed a card and sent in to the emergency ward.

After about five minutes' wait, a young intern took a quick look at the arm and sent me upstairs to the X-ray laboratory with a form specifying the picture he wanted. The X-ray technician was ready almost immediately, and in twenty minutes I was handed the developed plate to take back to the emergency ward. A fracture specialist took a look at the film and found I had a chipped elbow. It could, he said, heal upon its own in a sling, but I should return to the regular fracture clinic next morning. When I showed up for this second examination the pain had become intense. The head of the clinic ordered the elbow placed in a cast, and the pain stopped almost at once.

Two weeks later the cast was removed at the clinic and another X-ray taken. The next week a third X-ray was taken. After each reading the specialist assured me that although I could not yet straighten the elbow fully, it was healing all right. Special treatment, he said, might merely "seize" the joint rather than speed its return to normal—which, with time, it has done. At no time was anything I might have needed for the elbow not forthcoming. Perhaps the emergency clinic doctor should have ordered a cast immediately instead of letting me wait until the next morning; but that was a matter of medical opinion. On the whole the care I received free could not have been simpler or better.

To an American, the most refreshing thing about my treatment was the fact that I was never asked to pay for it. I know, of course, that virtually any hospital in the United States would give a similar kind of emergency care; but the problem of money would come up sooner or later. In Britain you don't pay, no matter who you are or how complicated your problem is or how long you have to stay in the hospital. Anyone who has a heart attack or appendicitis or an automobile accident can walk (or be carried) into any hospital and receive complete care free.

"Free treatment for foreigners" has been one aspect of the National Health Service frequently criticized by Conservatives in Commons. No doubt there have been some abuses, like Frenchmen coming over from Calais to get free false teeth or eyeglasses in Dover. But the simple fact is that once having decided on "free medical care for all," it is cheaper to treat anybody and everybody than to set up a complicated screening system to make sure each patient has a "right" to Health Service care.

The French, for example, have a monstrously clumsy state health insurance scheme whereby (after endless bureaucratic forms and records and payments) you pay your own bills and then claim restitution from the state. The British pay the whole cost out of taxes, provide the Health Service free, and have managed to keep bookkeeping and administrative records at a minimum.

How Socialized Medicine Works

To acquire a family physician in Britain, you go to the local post office for a list of Health Service doctors practicing in the area. You may sign up with any of them, and you can change if you aren't satisfied. Likewise the doctor is free to turn you down if he feels he already has enough patients on his panel list. When he accepts you, your name goes to a central registration file maintained to see that patients are signed up with only one doctor at a time. If you should need hospitalization, surgery, or special consultations, your doctor will make the arrangements for you to receive these services just as he would in private practice.

A physician may have a maximum of 3,500 patients on his panel. The average is about 2,200. He is paid a capitation fee of 18 shillings a year (about $2.65) for each patient plus an extra 12 shillings ($1.68) for every patient from number 501 to number 1,500. Hospital surgeons, consultants, and specialists are paid salaries graded according to skill. There is a system of "distinction grants" for particularly qualified men. Grants or interest-free loans are also made to individual physicians or groups to get started in practice or improve their offices. All National Health Service doctors, consultants, surgeons, etc., are equally free to take private fee-paying patients along with their state-paid patients.

The average net income after expenses of general practitioners in Britain is about £2,500—or around $7,000 a year. Before the war it was less than £1,000, though taxes were much lower and the pound then worth $4 as compared to $2.80 now. By British standards, physicians are fairly well paid today. Nevertheless they are dissatisfied with the Health Service salary structure, and a Royal Commission is now investigating it.

There is no registration system for free dental care. You simply make an appointment with a National Health Service dentist of your choice. He is paid a fixed fee by the state for routine work and passes you on to a specialist for complicated dentures or oral surgery.

Utopian as it sounds, this is exactly how the Health Service works in Britain today. For the patient, of course, the ultimate test is not how smoothly the system works but how good the medical care turns out to be.

To this question there is no easy answer. There have been plenty of bad experiences—frustrations, tragedies, and tempers shortened by the problems of conforming to a state machine. But to begin with, paying a doctor a fee does not automatically make him a good doctor—any more than free medical care makes bad doctors.

The Quality of Care

In a sense the National Health Service has created difficulties for itself by giving people the right to demand and expect medical treatment they never would have thought of buying out of their own pockets. As a result many of the criticisms of the Health Service have nothing to do with the merits of "socialized medicine *versus* private medicine." In the old days of medical charity, most people were not in a position to complain about their doctors. Today, however, in the House of Commons question hour members of Parliament regularly belabor the Minister of Health on behalf of aggrieved citizens seeking redress of Health Service mistakes.

For example, there was the case of a middle-aged man with rheumatoid arthritis in Pembrokeshire in the extreme west of Wales. His doctor decided that hospital treatment was required and arranged for an ambulance under the Health Service to drive the patient—a stretcher case—to the nearest hospital specializing in arthritic ailments. It was two hundred miles away. But when the man arrived the hospital refused to admit him, on the ground that they only handled ambulatory cases, and that the doctor had made a mistake in sending them a bedridden patient. So he was driven all the way back to Pembroke and became violently ill on the way.

His M.P. took the matter up with the Ministry of Health. In due course, the Minister wrote that "frankly the National Health Service let the patient down and we offer our sincere apologies and sympathies. While it will not be of much comfort to him, I am sure you will wish to know that steps have been taken to prevent such a mishap in future."

This incident was typical of many—a patient desperately in need of care and a heartlessly rigid interpretation of the rules by a hospital. However, it is also a fact that ten years ago a poor Welshman far out in the Pembroke countryside would never have dreamed of hiring an ambulance to take him two hundred miles to a special hospital.

Herein is the dilemma in assessing the quality of medicine under the National Health Service: once it is accepted that a modern democratic society has a responsibility for providing free medical care for all its citizens, certain standards inevitably change. They will fall for some people but will rise for many others.

The analogy is state-supported free education (which, incidentally, nobody todays calls "socialism"). Obviously private schools can offer smaller classes, greater individual attention, less standardization, and wider curricula. Private education is open to those who want it and can afford it. But the state goes on trying to improve its own system of education—and so it is with health and medicine in Britain today.

What Irks the Doctors

In trying to sort out the main lines of dissatisfaction with the National Health Service, I find that they revolve around inconveniences or frustrations rather than a basic indictment of the system or the principle. Physicians complain chiefly about "frivolous calls from patients." This was best described to me by a doctor who is one of the six hundred who stayed out of the service in 1948. He still had a successful private practice in London, although he knows the problems of many of his professional colleagues who, of course, practice under National Health.

"The worst of it is what I would call the 'aggressive attitude' of patients toward the doctor," he said. "Because a patient does not have to think twice about his condition before getting on to the doctor, he is at the doctor constantly to do all sorts of things which would perfectly well work themselves out. Then if he doesn't get a prescription or something he thinks the doctor isn't looking after him properly.

"This crowds the doctor's office, and leads to very superficial examination. The leisurely and thorough examination of a patient who may genuinely be in danger has broken down under the National Health Service. Instead—because any doctor can prescribe the most expensive sort of antibiotics free under the Health Service—there is a tendency simply to have a quick look and then let the umbrella of antibiotic drugs take care of the rest, partly in order to satisfy the patient that he's being well looked after.

"After a day of this sort of routine, when a doctor is bothered by frivolous night calls from patients expecting him to come running for no really good reason, his own patience and temper are ready to snap—and the whole process of medical care, and of good doctor-patient relationships breaks down."

This pretty much sums up the chief complaint of general practitioners in Britain (though it does not mean that doctors and patients are constantly snapping and snarling at each other here).

An independent analysis of doctors' grievances was made some months ago, by an American professor of economics from the Wharton School of the University of Pennsylvania, Dr. Paul F. Gemmill. He spent seven months in Britain probing the Health Service like a good old-fashioned leg-work reporter. His study of the Health Service was, he explains, "not for it, or against it, but *of* it." There was no official sponsorship of his inquiry, and as an American he might well be expected to hear all the gripes as well as the good. His method was simply to drop in unannounced at doctors' offices, and sit with the patients until all had been seen (observing waiting time as he waited), and then present himself and his questions to the physician.

He saw almost 400 doctors, and if there was no time for dis-cussion he left a questionnaire to be returned to him in Philadel-phia. He also left questionnaires with 1,500 National Health

Service patients. The results, it seems fair to say, are about the most straightforward survey to date of the private opinions of doctors and patients about the Health Service.

On the question of frivolous calls, he found that 49 per cent of the doctors said they "often" had time taken up with minor ailments, 30 per cent said "occasionally," and only 21 per cent said "almost never." On the other hand, he also asked if prompt visits and early examination enabled them to catch disease early, to which 11 per cent replied "often," 60 per cent replied "occasionally" and only 21 per cent "almost never." In summary, 79 per cent thought they were bothered by frivolous calls, while 71 per cent found that early visits helped to head off disease.

Paper work under the Health Service has been another doctor criticism. Dr. Gemmill found that only 39 per cent found it "burdensome" while the other 61 per cent said it was not. Both sides agreed that the National Health Service had increased certain kinds of form filling, but that it was largely offset by no longer having to make out bills and prod patients for private fees.

As to the burden of practice, with an average of 2,200 patients each, 59 per cent of the Health Service doctors find it "reasonably easy" to give adequate care to their panel lists, 38 per cent find it "difficult," but only a minute 3 per cent said it was "impossible."

The Hospital Bottleneck

The patients' complaints fit mainly under the heading, "We wait, wait, wait." If fewer people went to the doctor with "frivolous calls," waiting time would be cut and doctors would have less to complain about. But there is no real answer to waiting time except more facilities, and this again is not so much a complaint *against* the National Health Service as it is a *result* of it.

Of the 1,500 patients Dr. Gemmill queried, 37 per cent said they were getting better medical care than they did before 1948, 50 per cent said it was about the same, and only 13 per cent found it worse.

The greatest problem of waiting has been in the hospitals, which is essentially a matter of government policy. In the first five years of the Health Service, all its resources went to improve existing hospital facilities, or other priority needs. In 1955, the first new hospital in England for seventeen years was completed; ten more are now being built and six are in the final planning stage. In addition thirty hospitals will be modernized and expanded in 1959-1960. Thus after a very long lapse, a hospital program is now under way.

The hospital waiting-time problem has led to the rise of private health insurance which pays for special hospital beds, insuring, as it were, preferential treatment at extra charge within the National Health system. Since 1948 the number of people covered by such schemes has soared from 84,000 to 834,000.

For the doctors, a main trend of the last ten years has been into group practice—which the Ministry of Health encourages with special grants to build and equip clinics, and which, with the increasing complications of modern medicine, is regarded as the answer to the problem of the overworked general practitioners.

There are now 13,000 physicians in group practice in Britain —or 67 per cent of those engaged in general medical work. They may include a general practitioner and colleagues specializing in heart, ear-nose-throat, or other combinations. They pool their panel lists and fees and the expense of secretarial help, and in the aggregate can probably give better collective service to their patients than they could individually.

The cost of the National Health Service is a major target of its critics. Certainly it has far exceeded the original estimates, and certainly it has risen steadily, even astronomically. Partly this was due to the general inflation in Britain. In any case, it has now leveled off and is budgeted at a lower figure this year than last. Moreover the cost has fallen each year in terms of percentage of gross national product (less than 3.5 per cent this year), and in terms of cost per head of population it is ludicrously low.

This year the Ministry of Health estimates that about £750 million will be spent—partly by the national treasury, partly by local health authorities, partly in charges to the public such as the nominal one-shilling (13-cent) service charge on prescriptions. With just over 50 million people in England, Scotland, and Wales, this works out at £15 per head—or less than $50 per person for complete medical and hospital care.

Doctor Bills Are Gone Forever

Perhaps the most impressive achievement of the National Health Service after ten years is in "provision of care." For example, in 1948, with private practice pulling doctors into more prosperous areas, 60 per cent of the people of Britain were living in what the Ministry of Health regarded as "under-doctored areas." Today a doctor gets the same fee whether he treats a coal miner or a bank manager, and only 18 per cent of the people now live in under-doctored areas. In this decade, the total number of doctors in the United Kingdom has increased from 36,500 to over 49,000. Even though hospital building is only starting, 30,000 hospital beds have already been added through enlargement and improvement of existing facilities.

Nobody would claim that the National Health Service alone is responsible for improved health and mortality statistics. New drugs and medical discoveries would have produced improvement no matter what the system.

Nevertheless, deaths from tuberculosis in Britain have dropped from 23,076 in 1947 to 4,784 in 1957. Notification of TB cases has fallen from 47,000 to 33,000. In the same period, infant mortality per 1,000 live births is down from 41 to 23.1, while infant mortality after four weeks of life has fallen from 22.7 to 16.5 per 1,000. Life expectancy has risen to sixty-nine years for men and seventy-four years for women.

But beyond statistics there is the conviction . . . that the country is simply *healthier,* that far less time is being lost from work, that energy and vitality are much improved, and that in terms of man-hours of production the Health Service has a value to the

nation which can never be measured or defined. Granting that
food and living conditions are much improved as against ten
years ago, Mr. Macleod still believes the Health Service has
played a large part.

Still another intrinsic social gain has been made by the
British people. A medical tragedy can no longer become a
financial disaster. In Britain the shadow of medical bills has
been removed from family life forever.

For the middle classes here—with narrow budgets and little
opportunity for increased incomes—this is perhaps the most
significant result of the quiet social revolution which the Labour
government carried out in Britain from 1945 to 1951. The rich
could afford any kind of medicine and the poor were always
taken care of. The middle class, which could not plead poverty
and could not stand great medical expenses, faced the worst
problem when serious illness struck.

The National Health Service as it is working in Britain today
affords a maximum of individual freedom to both doctors and
patients. Most of the settled families of the country are signed
up with the same doctor they had in the old days—only now
he is paid by the state and they have no more doctor's bills. The
middle class needed the Health Service the most, and the middle
class has profited the most. An American cannot live in Britain
today and see the Health Service at work without coming to a
simple realization: what has been done here by democratic processes in a free society is a great step forward and an object
lesson for democracy throughout the world.

YOUTHS LEAVE BRITAIN [6]

College Polls Show Nearly Half "Want Out"

Now the British have something new to worry about. As
one Englishman expresses it:

"The brains are leaving the country."

[6] From article in *U.S. News & World Report.* 42:100+. Mr. 8, '57. Reprinted from *U.S. News & World Report,* an independent weekly news magazine
published at Washington. Copyright 1957 United States News Publishing Corporation.

At the present rate, more than 300,000 Britons will turn their backs on England this year. And a series of unofficial surveys shows that a surprisingly high proportion of them are scientists, engineers, teachers and skilled workers.

A poll conducted recently among Cambridge University students by the campus newspaper, *Varsity,* indicates clearly what is going on. Nearly half of the second- and third-year students who answered a questionnaire said they have decided to emigrate, or are thinking about doing so. A similar poll at Bristol University showed that an even higher percentage of students there wants to settle outside Britain after graduation. The editor of the Cambridge newspaper, commenting on the poll in a letter to the London *Economist,* says:

"We feel that the loss of one tenth of the future leaders of Britain is of the utmost gravity."

How poll went. In the Cambridge poll, questionnaires were sent to 450 representative students in their second and third years. Replies were made by 337 men students and 47 women.

To the question, "Have you decided to emigrate when you have graduated?" 11.3 per cent of the men and 34.1 per cent of the women replied, "Yes."

To the question, "If not, are you considering doing so?" 27.6 per cent of the men and 14.9 per cent of the women replied, "Yes."

Nearly 45 per cent of those who said they had already decided to emigrate or were considering doing so are scientists.

The poll at Bristol University drew 571 replies from a student body of 2,871. Here are the questions and answers:

"Do you intend to emigrate when you graduate?" "Yes," answered 24.2 per cent of the men and 13.4 per cent of the women.

"Are you considering emigrating when you graduate?" "Yes," said 27.2 per cent of the men and 15.1 per cent of the women.

"Are you satisfied with your chances in this country?" "No," replied 38.5 per cent of the men and 31.3 per cent of the women.

Too many restrictions. Why are so many students thinking of leaving this country? Lack of opportunity in Britain is the explanation of most of the Cambridge students who took part in the poll. Here is a typical comment by one who has decided to leave:

"England is too restricted by regulations, trade unions and general apathy of the majority of the people. New blood is welcome, but not new ideas. I want to go to a country where both are equally needed so that I can give something to that country, rather than just live off it."

The Cambridge poll is being challenged by some experts because of the smallness of the sample—less than 10 per cent of the 5,603 second- and third-year students at the school. But officials at the University's employment office indicate that job applications tend to confirm the poll. More and more students express interest in jobs outside England.

Adding to growing concern of the country over losing too many of its best-educated young people and the most skilled of its young workers is an unofficial survey of the thousands of people who line up every day outside the Commonwealth immigration offices in London.

That survey revealed that 60 per cent of the men seeking to move to Canada, Australia or the other Commonwealth countries are between the ages of twenty and fifty-five—the most productive age group. An additional 30 per cent are under twenty years of age. Fewer than 10 per cent are older than fifty-five.

Canada reports that a majority of those settling there from Britain are young professional people—engineers, technicians, scientists, doctors, accountants, and teachers—along with skilled workers. An official of the British Ministry of Education, remarking on this trend, says:

"I used to encourage young men and women with a sense of adventure and the desire to get ahead to go to Canada. They no longer need encouragement. So many want to leave that it may well become a source of embarrassment to us.". . .

There is no hiding the growing concern among government officials and businessmen over the fact that a high proportion of those moving out are professional people and skilled workers. Now, if the polls are correct, a big share of the university students is ready to join this exodus from Britain.

II. THE CONTEMPORARY FABRIC

EDITOR'S INTRODUCTION

In many ways the situation and problems that Britain faces today are not unique to that country, nor are they new. Essentially they are further results of industrialization and its concomitants—the wider distribution of income, educational opportunity, and leisure. But the combination of these problems has been peculiar to postwar Britain as they have operated against a background of waning imperial and commercial power in a country heavily dependent on world trade.

The long period of Conservative party rule in a time of major change is one of the remarkable aspects of postwar British politics. Since the war, Britain has had six years of Labour and ten years of Conservative party rule. The next elections do not have to be called by the Prime Minister until 1964, by which time the Conservatives will have been in power for an almost unprecedented thirteen-year period. The postwar years therefore split into the period from 1945 to 1951 when Labour, under the leadership of Prime Minister Clement Attlee, had a majority in the House of Commons, and the years since the latter date, when the Conservatives have been in power. Winston Churchill took office in 1951, following the victory of the Conservatives at the polls, and stepped down in April 1955, when Anthony Eden took his place.

Eden was forced to resign in 1957 as a result of the failure of the attempt to occupy the Suez Canal zone in October-November 1956 following the nationalization of the canal by Egypt. The British and French found to their dismay that their armed forces could not rapidly overrun the zone, but—far more important—they discovered that they could not rely on the United States for support in all possible circumstances. For practically the only time during the 1950's, Russia and America found themselves on the same side of a major political issue.

In addition, most of the Commonwealth quietly deplored or actively condemned the Suez action. Finally, a very large proportion of the British people felt the action was stupid or worse.

The new Prime Minister, Harold Macmillan, who took office early in 1957, had to rebuild the prestige of the United Kingdom. By this time certain limitations on the future role of the United Kingdom had been made dramatically clear. The inability of France and Britain to go it alone without the United States, even if they were themselves united, had been graphically illustrated. The philosophy of Macmillan, which accepts a second-ranking position, is made clear in the initial article of this section, which comments on the 1959 general election. The next two articles examine the general aims and philosophies of the Conservative and Labour parties at the beginning of the 1960's and provide an explanation of the present popularity of the Conservatives.

As the article "Slow Economic Progress" shows, Britain's growth in the postwar years has been far slower than that of most other Western countries. Nevertheless, there has been considerable progress toward a high standard of living in England as elsewhere in Europe: "The Economy" groups Britain with Denmark, Switzerland, and other continental nations as second only to the United States and Canada in national income per person.

Britain's economy poses the same problems as do many other industrial societies with a high standard of living. The last five articles in this section deal with problems analogous to those in the United States. "Town Planning in London" discusses the impact of the automobile on patterns of living. In the next selection, Norman MacKenzie points out some basic factors operating to cause recent racial tensions which have given the lie to the comfortable theory that the British do not, and could not, have a race problem. The remaining selections examine social problems on a wider scale. In Aidan Crawley's "The Affluent Society in Britain"—a title obviously borrowed from John Kenneth Galbraith's book—it is argued that because of the increased abundance of goods many of the old economic policies should be reversed. Anthony Sampson discusses the Americanization of business methods and spending habits. And in "The Irresponsible Society," Richard Titmuss complains that the effect of the increase in wealth has been to allow the newly well-off to ignore the social problems which still exist and argues that only a reversal of this trend will lead to the development of a suitable form of society.

POLITICS IN GREAT BRITAIN [1]

The Art of the Practical

Outside Conservative party headquarters in London's Smith Square, jubilant crowds stumbled over TV cables and shouted noisily at each new bulletin heralding the election of yet another Tory M.P. At 1:25 A.M., long after the Labourites at their glum command post across the square had conceded defeat in Britain's 1959 general election, an elegant gray-haired figure in evening dress stepped from a sedan to a surge of Tory cheers. "Well done, Mac," shouted voices. "You did it!" The tall, patrician-looking man paused for a moment, his handsome wife in blue evening gown at his side. "It has gone off rather well," murmured Prime Minister Harold Macmillan.

Marking 28 million x's on ballot papers that carried no mark of party affiliations but simply the names of their parliamentary candidates in 630 local constituencies, the voters of the British Isles last week gave Maurice Harold Macmillan, sixty-five, a smashing personal triumph in one of the most decisive and significant political battles of the postwar era. Macmillan had led his party to its third straight victory and doubled its majority in the House of Commons, a feat without parallel in the annals of of British politics. Overcoming a slashing Labour party challenge, he had won his own mandate to rule Britain for the next five years. He had won too, the right to speak for England. . .

[1] From "The Art of the Practical," *Time.* 74:33-8. O. 19, '59. Copyright Time Inc. 1959. Reprinted by permission.

and to conserve and expand the Tory-fostered prosperity that had cracked the class lines of British society and provided the votes for his victory. . . .

The box score of Macmillan's win:

	Seats		Millions of Votes	
	1959	1955	1959	1955
Tory	365	345	13.7	13.3
Labour	258	277	12.2	12.4
Liberal	6	6	1.6	.7

Thus, a swing to the Tories of a small fraction of the British electorate in marginal constituencies was enough to jump their Commons majority from 53 to 100 seats. Liberals, on the strength of their 1,600,000 popular vote, forecast with eager optimism that they would soon succeed Labour as the chief opposition party—a prediction that overlooked the fact that more than 40 per cent of British voters stuck by Labour through the sweep. But the fact remained that for Britain's fifty-three-year-old Labour party it was a staggering defeat, threatening to open never-healed wounds, confronting Labour's leaders with the hard fact that Britain's citizens want no more socialism.

The man who fashioned this dramatic political triumph for Britain's Conservatives sports the languidly aristocratic look and the offhandedly arrogant air of a lordly old Tory of the style of Wellington and Disraeli. But behind the elaborately careless Edwardian manner that provokes both cheers and jeers for "Supermac" and "Macwonder," Harold Macmillan maintains a superbly efficient mastery of the political art of the practical. For all his proud Tory brows and mustache, Macmillan possesses an agile intelligence and free-ranging historical imagination that have enabled him to adjust cheerfully to the limits of Britain's present-day power, and to work to make his country the "senior junior partner in the Western alliance." And domestically, Macmillan is an unabashed pragmatist who looks to the right, borrows from the left, and walks grandly through the middle in the immemorial British tradition.

Against this formidable foe, Labour had waged an aggressive "We can do it better" campaign. This display of vigor, reinforced by the unexpectedly effective performance of Labour Leader Hugh Gaitskell, upset Tory plans for a quiet election and turned the three-week campaign into the toughest-talking election battle since Labour's 1945 victory over Winston Churchill. Said Labour's "Nye" Bevan: "I have seen the squint in [Macmillan's] soul." Macmillan himself, harking back to an old description of Hugh Gaitskell as "a desiccated calculating machine," gleefully cracked: "I still think he is rather desiccated, but his reputation as a calculator is gone with the wind. His promises are the gambler's last throw." "There have been a number of personal attacks on me," said Gaitskell, "but I don't complain." "I complain," Mrs. Gaitskell piped up. In his best parade-ground manner, Field Marshall Viscount Montgomery, no candidate but deep in the battle, barked: "Anybody who votes Labour should be locked up in a lunatic asylum." . . .

[One of the major advantages for Macmillan was the panorama of peace and prosperity which contrasted with the bitter confusion inherited from Sir Anthony Eden in the aftermath of the Suez invasion less than three years earlier.] Not since Winston Churchill took office as German armies poured across Western Europe had a British Prime Minister gone to Downing Street under more unhappy circumstances. [When Macmillan took office at the beginning of 1957] unemployment was rising at home, living costs were rocketing toward record heights, the pound faltered as gold and dollar reserves plunged to a five-year low. Internationally, Britain's prestige was at its lowest ebb in modern history. The United States had publicly repudiated Britain, the alliance was strained, President Eisenhower had quietly refused to invite Eden and his ministers to Washington. The Commonwealth itself, led by India and Canada, had condemned Britain's act of violence.

Moving into 10 Downing Street, Macmillan (who still proclaims, "I believe history will prove us right over Suez") posted a line from *The Gondoliers* on an office door: "Calm cool deliberation disentangles every knot." Detached, confident, unflappable, the new Prime Minister promptly began to operate on the premise that a cardinal point of British foreign policy nowadays is the amount of influence it can exert over U.S. foreign policy. Back in World War II, sent to North Africa on his first ministerial assignment by Winston Churchill, Macmillan had already accepted the inevitable British transition from senior to junior partner in the Atlantic alliance. "Never forget," he peptalked junior British officers at Eisenhower's North African headquarters, "that we are the Greeks in their Roman empire." Within five months after Suez, the Prime Minister with the proud Tory look was making the most of his wartime friendship with Ike, and of his own American blood (his mother was Helen Belles of Spencer, Indiana), to reestablish the alliance in a meeting with Ike in Bermuda.

The United States rift mended, Macmillan set out to repair his Commonwealth fences with a Far Eastern tour, astonished everybody by getting on splendidly with Nehru. ("I wonder if the Romans ever visited Britain after they left," asked History Buff Macmillan at Delhi.). . .

The Deflationist

To stop the deadly inflationary drift he faced on Britain's domestic front, Macmillan was ready to take bold risks. Clamping a tight credit pinch on the business economy, he forced the bank rate up to 7 per cent, the highest level in thirty-seven years. These daringly deflationary tactics brought on the heaviest unemployment Britain had known since World War II, and cost Macmillan's Tories by-election after by-election, but they effectively stalled the trade unions' drive for the annual round of handsome wage boosts.

By . . . [the spring of 1959] Macmillan's stern economic medicine was beginning to show results. When Labour M.P.'s noisily demanded a debate on unemployment, Iain Macleod was able to drive them to cover by producing figures showing that the number of jobless had shrunk to 1.9% of Britain's labor force.

The Silver Spoon

Despite the dramatic revolution he has worked in Britain's economic fortunes, Harold Macmillan is still not every Englishman's cup of tea. Though he assiduously keeps alive the memory of his grandfather, a Scottish tenant farmer who in 1843 walked penniless into London, there to found the publishing house of Macmillan and Company, Ltd., Harold Macmillan himself was born with a silver spoon in his mouth. Endowed with the best upper-class English education (Eton and Oxford), he served as a company officer with the elite Grenadier Guards during World War I—in which he was three times wounded. Soon after the war he married Lady Dorothy Cavendish, daughter of the Duke of Devonshire, thereby acquired bonds with most of England's remaining great Tory families.

With his country-squire manner, his tweedy attire, and his speech so casual and so polished as to invite suspicion that it has been rehearsed, Macmillan sometimes reminds his countrymen of Walter Savage Landor's lines: "I strove with none, for none was worth my strife." Even a Tory sympathizer, watching Macmillan on television a fortnight ago, found himself "suddenly and strangely aware of an awful feeling of class consciousness." But those who have listened to and watched Macmillan longest remain unimpressed by such nuances, remember instead that he is a shrewd business executive and, above all, a supreme politician. . . .

Macmillan gets the best out of his ministers and civil servants by keeping hands off their departments, taking pains to parcel out praise for good jobs, but not so profusely that the coin is devalued. An early riser, he tackles state papers as early as 6 A.M., works with such dispatch that seven secretaries, arriving at 10, find their in-boxes stuffed with documents, some inscribed with marginal notes in red ink, others with summaries of the Prime Minister's views or orders. "Things are never on top of him; he is on top of them," said one secretary.

Suave in a large crowd, shy in a small one, Macmillan is really at home only in the professional, forensic atmosphere of the House of Commons, in the tweedy domesticity of his Sussex country place, or in the intimate company of a few . . . [upper-class] friends. . . .

For Labour, Macmillan's triumph was a defeat so harsh and decisive that it posed a real question as to whether the party could survive in its present form. Hard as Hugh Gaitskell had fought to moderate the dated dogmas of socialism, the Labour party had not been able to shake off the unpopular name of nationalization, the unhappy memory of postwar austerity or the unforgiving fetters of narrow trade union interests.

"We still represent nearly half of the nation," cried Gaitskell doggedly after the election. "We shall attack again and again until we win." This was brave talk, but if Hugh Gaitskell continued to pursue his policy of moderation, he would run a real risk of driving Labour's doctrinaire left wing into secession from the party. . . .

For Britain the decisive election verdict ended, for all practical purposes, the threat of renationalization of the steel industry, and opened the way for a new flow of capital into the United Kingdom, already the No. 1 country in Europe for U.S. investment. The Tory sweep also cleared the decks for the economic expansion that will have to come if Britain, whose strength derives from trade, is to regain from Germany its place as the world's second trading nation. . . .

No less important to Britain's future, however, are such social goals as the Tory program to step up slum clearance and rehouse a million more Britons by 1965. For Harold Macmillan, such programs are both ethical and practical imperatives. As he sees it, the guiding principle of Tory democracy must be that laid down by his favorite predecessor, Benjamin Disraeli: "To elevate the condition of the people." It is by elevating the condition of the people that Macmillan has led the British electorate steadily away from the sterile, Socialist doctrines that once threatened to emasculate the free economy that is Britain's best hope for the future. In an electorate whose workers have become middle class, said Macmillan in a TV victory speech . . . , "the class war is obsolete." Then, with that faintly superior smile, he added: "Nowadays it is ungrammatical but true to say that 'us' are 'they' and 'they' are 'us.' "

THE BRITISH TORY—FAR FROM TORY [2]

The Palace of Westminster, where new models in politicians are assessed with the interest Detroit gives to the latest cars or Paris to the newest fashions, is in the sixth month of a long analytical look at the new Tories. These political technicians dominate Prime Minister Macmillan's government which, in turn, will dominate British politics for five years—and, unless the Labour party wakes up, probably for five more after that.

Since 1945 the Conservative party in this country has undergone a gentlemanly, almost genteel, revolution. Like all revolutions, this one pushed to the top a new group of leaders. These now provide the driving force in the Conservative government, both in the Cabinet and among the junior ministers, those assistant executive vice presidents of British politics.

Let us look at one of them, "Mr. MacMarkinson," as he addresses the House of Commons from the Government front bench. He speaks not in the accents of Eton and Oxford [the traditional status educational institutions] but in standard BBC [the accent used by announcers for the government-owned radio and television system], with just a faint touch of some more earthy origin, the industrial North, perhaps, or the money-grubbing Midlands. He is clad in the sober dark suit suitable to a Minister of the Crown, but he is a little rumpled, he lacks elegance. His tie, if it is a school tie, is that of a public school but of a rather undistinguished one, hardly Eton or Harrow or

[2] From article by Drew Middleton, chief of the London bureau of the New York *Times*. New York *Times Magazine*. p 12+. Ap. 17, '60. Reprinted by permission.

Winchester. His speech is eminently practical, full of figures, which he cites accurately, but without the oratorical grace notes of an earlier generation of Tories.

Big Ben tolls 5:30. At just that hour, all over Britain, men very much like "Mr. MacMarkinson" are bellying up to saloon bars for a drink. In background, upbringing and outlook he is very much like them. That is his strength. He does not speak for the new Conservatives. He is one.

To the surviving old-time Conservatives throughout the country, he is a difficult, even—at certain times and on certain issues, an odious fellow. But he wins. He keeps "those Bolshies" on the Labour side out of office.

However, to traditionalists, he is a sad comedown from sprigs of the nobility like Churchill or titled aristocrats . . . or the spokesmen for the great industrial interests who, until 1945, dominated the party. These, with their long tradition of government and diplomacy, their expansive habits of thought and life, were followed and admired instinctively by the people who then made up the rank and file of the party.

Churchill (after he had been welcomed back into the fold), . . . Salisbury and the rest had an innate appeal to the red-faced ex-majors, formidable dowagers and sporting farmers who ran the local constituency parties. It was one of the dowagers who excited the 1945 conference of the party by announcing she had a genuine treat for the audience, "a real Conservative trade unionist." Between 3.5 and 4 million trade unionists, perhaps more, voted for the Conservatives in the last general election.

The word "conservative" has a warm, reassuring sound to those on the right in politics. It means a party that is safe and predictable. But it is unwise to compare Mr. Macmillan's Conservatives with Mr. Eisenhower's Republicans. In their attitude toward the control of the economy, toward the pressing problems in Africa, toward a *détente* with the Soviet Union, British Conservatives are well to the left of American Republicans. By American standards many of the policies they adopt and almost all the policies they discuss are radical.

There is no desire on the part of voters or leaders to return to the Britain of before the war, save in a few areas in the South that retain vestigial remains of the old-time conservatism. . . .

The new leaders have led the Tories into paradoxical policies and radical solutions because they understand that Britain's present economic and strategic position in the world makes a return to the old conservatism suicidal alike for the party and for the country. They may cast admiring, even wishful glances at Republicans bellowing the joys of unrestricted individual enterprise, but they know that such joys are not for Britain in her present position.

They are willing to impose economic controls, gently exercised, unobtrusive, but still controls, that would strike their opposite numbers in Washington as socialism. For they know, and even their most hidebound voters are slowly learning, that Britain's economy eternally balances on a knife edge and that controls can keep it from falling off. Is the country spending too much on itself to the detriment of the export trade? Then use the government budget to reduce imports. "Conservative freedom works," say the campaign orators. But only so much freedom and only at certain times.

This is anathema to unreconstructed Tories. But it is modern conservatism's approach. The Conservatives give the electorate the impression of knowing just where and when to tinker with the vast, complicated machinery of the economy so that it keeps progressing steadily, and the television masts sprout like Iowa corn throughout the kingdom.

This impression of progress does the utmost damage to the Labour party. For Labour, both in internal affairs and in international policies, seems to stand still. In many respects the views of some of its leaders, often those who have the loudest voices and the biggest audiences, do not seem to have changed in a quarter of a century. They, not the Conservatives, appear to resist fresh ideas.

Although Hugh Gaitskell tries to waken the sleepers, the party still dreams of the angry thirties. Nationalization, how much and what for, is still a major issue among the activists of the Labour party—and perhaps nowhere else in Britain. At the slightest opportunity the Spanish civil war or the horrors of Auschwitz are raised as rallying cries to the Labour faithful.

Labour would like to believe that the Conservative political boom was fostered by Britain's economic boom. Perhaps. But the Conservatives also are doing things in a forceful, novel manner. They are bringing in new schemes for nuclear power and highways, changing the map of Africa and flying off to see Mr. Khrushchev or Mr. Eisenhower. And they are doing it with men very like the up-and-coming young businessmen or the factory workers who are moving to more responsible jobs in the new industries.

The Tories admit they are pragmatic. They reject the opposition's charge that they are unprincipled.

"Look," said one of "Mr. MacMarkinson's" colleagues, "when we came in in 1951 this country was in a hell of a hole. We had to be flexible and adaptable. Of course, we've accepted some Labour ideas. Why not? The country needed them. We'll use anything we can to get to our main goal, a reasonably stable economy and a country that, as a result, counts for something again." . . .

His words emphasize another difference with Labour. The modern Conservative party is refreshingly free of dogma. And it is dogma, inherited from the cloth-cap era of British socialism, that chains the Labour party to policies suitable to the 1930's but ridiculous in Britain today.

When the great row opened in the Labour ranks over Gaitskell's attempt to modernize the party constitution, Tories unanimously admitted that Gaitskell was on the right track. "But they'll tear him apart," one minister said. "And they'll wind up with a compromise. They've been asleep too long. Thank God we don't have a constitution in our party.". . .

Britain today is undergoing an economic change similar to that which struck the United States in the 1920's. Goods, services, luxuries long out of reach are coming within the grasp of the great mass of the working class. The new industries have fathered a new class, part manual worker, part technician, part businessman. The breakup of the urban concentrations of population has sent millions out of the cities into new communities and real homes.

The new conservatism suits the majority in this group because its policies seem designed not to disturb them. These voters, like "Mr. MacMarkinson" and his colleagues, have no desire to return to the glories of Georgian or Edwardian Britain. In fact, the conservatism of those days, based on economic resources now out of reach and strategic considerations no longer important, seems slightly outdated. Britain is back to the simple faith of Lord Palmerston:

"We have no eternal allies and no perpetual enemies; our interests are eternal, and those interests it is our duty to follow."

"We all heard that fellow MacMarkinson on the telly the other night. Not like toffee-nosed Tory, you know, just like one of the blokes at the works. Knows we have to move with the times. Can't keep worrying about the past. No future in that."

ENGLAND'S LABOUR PARTY [3]

Ever since its birth sixty years ago, the British Labour party has appeared to be on the point of collapse. Again and again, the mourners have assembled in the graveyard—only to find the prospective corpse dancing merrily on top of the coffin. Over the years Labour politicians have developed uncanny skill at plunging their daggers into each other's backs, hard enough to wound but not to kill. The Labour movement has stumbled on, raucous, quarrelsome, undignified—but splendidly alive. But now it seems to have ground to a halt. Labour has lost three elections in a row; and the party is split down the middle. It may yet recover: stranger things have happened in British history. But short of a miracle it is hard to see how it can escape a devastating civil war, from which it must emerge severely crippled, if not actually destroyed.

[3] From "England's Labor Party and Its Discontents" by David Marquand, journalist on the staff of the Manchester *Guardian*. Reprinted from *Commentary*. 30:489-96. D. '60. Copyright American Jewish Committee. Reprinted by permission.

Many Labour members of Parliament would deny this. They cannot deny that the Labour party conference at Scarborough early in October [1960] rejected the defense policy prepared by the Executive, though it made more concessions to the left than any previous defense platform had done: it recognized that an independent British nuclear deterrent is not possible; demanded that NATO should reduce its dangerous dependence on tactical nuclear weapons; warned of the spread of nuclear weapons to other countries; and called for reforms in the structure of the Western alliance. But it clearly and explicitly reaffirmed its belief in the continued necessity of the alliance—and it was evidently this that the majority would not accept. Yet the majority was a small one, and the vote defeating the Executive policy was, in fact, less than representative. The conference rejected "any defense policy based on the threat of the use of tactical or strategic nuclear weapons" by a vote of 3,282,000 to 3,239,000; it demanded the "unilateral renunciation of the manufacture, stockpiling and basing of nuclear weapons in Great Britain" by a vote of only 3,303,000 to 2,836,000. . . . Hence, it is said by some optimists, the crisis is only temporary.

Temporary it may be: but to an outsider, at least, it looks certain to last much longer than just a year. The "unilateralist" resolutions were passed in open defiance of the party leader and against the advice of the party's chief spokesmen on foreign affairs and defense. In the course of his speech, Hugh Gaitskell declared that if the vote went against him, he would "fight, fight, and fight again" to reverse it. He has carried out his threat, supported by two thirds of his Labour colleagues in Parliament. Yet according to the party constitution, the final authority for policy making lies with the annual conference; and the rift has already provoked open strife in the parliamentary party. . . .

But even if the next party conference should reverse the Scarborough decision, would that really be the end of the matter? The split in the Labour party is a fundamental one, not confined to foreign affairs and defense. Scarborough was only the last and noisiest of a series of explosions. When Labour went out of office in 1951, it was already split over the rearmament program made necessary by the Korean war. In 1954, the rift was deepened still further by the implications of German rearmament. For a short time in 1955 the then leader of the party's left wing—Aneurin Bevan—was actually suspended from the parliamentary group. After Gaitskell's election to the leadership in 1955, there was a brief, unconvincing, and unconsummated honeymoon between the left and the right. Bevan and Gaitskell made peace, and the divisions in the party were temporarily buried. But an acute listener could still detect subterranean rumbles, and from time to time the volcano seemed on the point of erupting once again. During the election campaign in the fall of 1959, it is true, the party seemed more united than at any time in the last fifteen years; and Gaitskell's leadership was apparently accepted in the most unlikely quarters with something approaching enthusiasm. But after the election defeat, Gaitskell's reputation came crashing down; the old volcano did erupt—and it was found that the molten lava had lost none of its heat.

The election defeat itself was partly to blame for this. British politics is a cruel sport, in which the captain of a losing team must expect to be kicked to death by his own side. To vary the metaphor, there is a tribal quality about British political parties: so long as the tribe is on top, its chief is revered and given a great deal of power. But let the tribe run into a period of bad luck, and the chief is liable to end in the cook-pot. British history offers only one parallel to the Labour party's recent record of three defeats in a row: the three defeats suffered by the Conservatives between 1906 and 1914. Prolonged failure has led to schism and rebellion. Balfour, the Conservative leader, received the same ferocious treatment from right-wing Tories that Gaitskell has been getting lately from left-wing Socialists. Labour's defeat in last year's elections was in no sense Gaitskell's fault—without him, in fact, Labour would almost certainly have fared worse. Yet Gaitskell's troubles have been aggravated by his personality. Successful British politicians, it has been said, must be in character either bishops or bookmakers. Gladstone was a bishop. Disraeli was a bookmaker. Harold Macmillan is one of the most polished and versatile bookmakers in our recent history.

Gaitskell is neither. He is a university don. He lacks the flaming moral passion of the bishop—and he lacks, even more disastrously, the tactical agility of the bookmaker. During the past year, the most critical in his party's history, he has made almost no effort to stump the country for his policies, and he has taken stubborn delight in fighting his critics not where *they* are weakest, but where *he* is weakest. He is, moreover, the walking embodiment of Aristotle's "magnanimous man": reasonable, calm, virtuous—and a little stiff. In private he is said to be warm and emotional; in public the warmth is apt to be concealed beneath the armor plating of the British middle class. Indeed, Gaitskell as a politician is strangely reminiscent of Adlai Stevenson: he has all the gifts needed by a political leader—except being good at politics. Worst of all, he is a middle-class intellectual, and yet on the right wing of the party. One of the unwritten rules of Labour party politics is that intellectuals are allowed only on the left. Union leaders can safely stand on the right: they may be bitterly attacked, but they cannot be accused of patronizing the rest of the movement—whatever they do, they will be one of "us," not one of "them." But a middle-class intellectual is always apt to be suspect in a predominantly working-class party. If he takes care to present himself as a left-winger, in tune with the party's emotions, he can work his passage and win acceptance. But if his speeches contain more appeals to moderation and sanity than to passion and principle, he can easily sound like a prig or a snob—an outsider come to lecture, not an insider trying to persuade. . . .

The really important differences in the Labour party are at bottom ideological, not personal—though no one seems to know for certain what the ideological differences are about. The commonest way of describing them is to say that Labour is divided between a "doctrinaire" and a "pragmatic" wing. As a form of political shorthand, readily available to the editorial writer, this description has its merits, but it conceals more than it describes. What exactly is the doctrine which the "doctrinaires" hold so dear? No one knows: least of all they themselves. British socialism, unlike continental social democracy, has no sacred books.

It has always owed more to Methodism than to Marxism—and this is at least as true of the left as it is of the right. A few members of the left are, or have been, fellow-travelers, but even they are generally Christian Socialists gone soft, not full-blooded Marxists. And in any case, the vast majority of the left are not fellow-travelers at all. They may occasionally indulge in wishful thinking about the Soviet Union—but then they indulge in wishful thinking about everything.

If anyone in the Labour party has a doctrine, indeed, it is the intellectuals of the "pragmatic" right. During the past ten years, three British Socialists have produced writings of merit: Aneurin Bevan, John Strachey, and Anthony Crosland. Of the three, only Bevan belonged to the left wing of the party—and after reading his book, *In Place of Fear,* one is little the wiser about his theoretical beliefs. John Strachey is in a different category. His two volumes *(Contemporary Capitalism* and *The End of Empire)* are a real contribution to Socialist thought—and what is more, they are heavily influenced by Marx. But Strachey is no longer a left-winger; he supports Gaitskell and is firmly committed to NATO. Crosland is an even more revealing example. He is perhaps the most important ideologue of the right, and certainly the most creative of the younger intellectuals in the party. His book, *The Future of Socialism,* is massive and erudite as well as brilliant. But whatever else it may be, it is certainly not "pragmatic." A large section is occupied by an almost scholastic discussion on whether capitalism is still capitalism—or something else. Another section is occupied by an elaborate attempt to prove that almost every Socialist writer who ever lived really thought what Crosland thinks. Crosland himself is no more pragmatic than his book. He has insisted on his doctrine with the stubbornness of a Calvinist, and has given the impression that he would cheerfully destroy his political future rather than sacrifice his views.

The right, then, has its doctrines. But only the left has a Faith. That is the real difference between them. The left-wingers are the true descendants of the early pioneers, the Chartists of the nineteenth century, and the Levellers of the seventeenth. For them, the progress of political action is not to win power: it is to make a new heaven and a new earth. The left sometimes does not know what it is fighting for—but it always knows what it is fighting against. Its real enemy is the gray confusion of ordinary life, the tawdry compromises of practical politics, the inevitable pettiness of living people—all summed up in the single word, "capitalism." To the left, capitalism is not simply an economic system which evolves; one might as well suggest to a Presbyterian of the old school that the Devil evolves. Capitalism is incorrigible; and the changes that occasionally appear on its surfaces are simply camouflage to trap the unwary. To an outsider, the left's brand of socialism seems increasingly remote from the real world. To the faithful, it is the "old-time religion," immaculate and inviolable—and if the real world does not like it, that merely proves that the real world is corrupt. Mrs. Barbara Castle, chairman of the party last year, unconsciously revealed the fundamentalist psychology of the left in an address she made at the 1959 conference to a group which had met to consider the implications of the party's third successive electoral defeat. In the circumstances, even she might have admitted that perhaps all was not well with the party's Creed. On the contrary, her verdict was: "It is chasing fantasies to imagine that we can win elections on moral issues in a democracy built on such amoral foundations." That is, the electors aren't good enough for the Labour party! . . .

The strong ecclesiastical character of the Labour movement has never been better illustrated than by its current controversy about public ownership. The crucial clause of the party constitution, adopted in 1918 after years of effort by what was at first a minority of Socialists, runs as follows:

To secure for the workers by hand or by brain the full fruits of their industry and the most equitable distribution thereof that may be possible upon the basis of the common ownership of the means of production, distribution and exchange and the best obtainable system of popular administration and control of each industry or service.

This is the notorious "Clause 4" of the constitution, now colloquially known as the "Old Testament." After the party's defeat last year, Gaitskell tried to delete Clause 4 and substitute a broader statement of aims which would no longer commit the party to wholesale public ownership. His ostensible reason was tactical. "Nationalization" has become the favorite boo-word of British politics, guaranteed to torpedo the electoral hopes of any party that advocates it. So long as Clause 4 remains, Gaitskell's argument ran, the press will terrorize the electorate with the scarecrow of wholesale nationalization, and no matter how attractive the rest of Labour's program may be, the Conservatives will go on winning elections. Beneath this tactical argument there was, however, a theoretical assumption: the Labour party constitution was drawn up before Keynes had shattered the noble edifice of classical economics. To the early Socialists it seemed self-evident that the cycle of booms and slumps could only be eliminated by public ownership. Keynesian economics destroyed the assumptions on which this doctrine rested—and the experience of the postwar world appeared to show that Keynes was right. Governments, it seemed, could control the economy and maintain full employment without nationalization. But in that case, why nationalize?

That, in essence, was Gaitskell's question. True, Gaitskell and most of his supporters have never denied that public ownership can be a useful device for improving economic efficiency or preventing monopoly. But for the left, public ownership is far more than a useful device: it is the very essence of socialism. Gaitskell's assault on Clause 4 was greeted with rage. . . . The emotional reaction . . . crystallized into an argument, or rather two arguments.

The first, and somewhat unsophisticated, rejoinder was that the Labour party had lost three elections not because it was too Socialist but because it was not Socialist enough. The extreme left of the Labour party bears a suspicious resemblance to the extreme right of the Republican party in the United States: both appear to believe that the recipe for influencing electors is to tell them what they don't want to hear in the loudest possible voice. "Me-tooism," it was said, was the real curse of the Labour party. The electors would never vote for a party without the courage of its convictions. The only hope for Labour was to make a full-scale attack on "capitalism." Moreover, it was argued, the party workers saw no point in persuading their friends and neighbors to vote for a milk-and-water program. Gaitskell's timidity was sending these gallant shock troops to sleep. Only when they returned to the firing line could Labour hope to win.

The second argument, by contrast, was dazzling in its sophistication and audacity. As Mr. Richard Crossman sees it, radical governments only come to power in Britain if there is a real crisis. If Labour sneaked into power now, as a result of assiduous servility to the prejudices of the electorate, it would not be able to force through a really Socialist program. Power, in fact, is the last thing Labour should be seeking now. For in spite of Keynes, capitalism is heading for a catastrophe, different in origin from that prophesied by Marx—but similar in effect. If Labour resolutely rejects the temptations of vote-catching, if it plays the part of Cassandra and gives warning of the wrath to come, if above all it insists on the full rigor of socialism as the only solution—then when catastrophe does come, Labour will reap its reward. This approach was based on an unlikely foundation, the writings of John Kenneth Galbraith; for *The Affluent Society* has become the Bible of the left. Crossman claims that Galbraith has shown the apparent stability of contemporary capitalism to be a sham: economic power rests with the great oligopolies; the State may propose—the Organization Men dispose. Hence, "private opulence and public squalor"; hence the absence of adequate capital investment; hence the growing superiority of the Soviet Union—and hence the coming crisis.

These ideological differences are concerned chiefly with domestic politics. Yet the great conflicts which have periodically torn the Labour party to pieces in the last ten years have almost all been over foreign policy and defense. Nationalization, however fundamental its importance, has been a damp squib compared with the rearmament program, German rearmament, SEATO, and the H-bomb. Why? Is there any logical con-

nection between the left's stand on public ownership and its
foreign policy? Why should the battles over foreign policy
and defense have been so much the more savage?

There is, in fact, no logical connection, just as there is no
purely rational explanation for the greater bitterness of argument over foreign affairs. But the divisions in the party are
not based on reason alone: their source is emotional. To the
right, the object of political activity is to win power and carry
out piecemeal reforms. To the left, the object is utopia and
the method a crusade against evil—and of all evils, the evil of
war is the worst; of all utopias, the most attractive is a world
at peace, without conflict. . . .

In isolation, these ideological and emotional divisions, even
the divisions over foreign policy, might not matter. Unfortunately they have been superimposed on an already gloomy
situation. Since 1950, Labour has been swimming against the
sociological tide—and the knowledge that the tide was first set
in motion by the postwar Labour government does nothing to
sweeten the experience. The most obvious reason for Labour's
defeats is the growth in material prosperity. In the past decade,
parts of Britain have entered the age of mass consumption—
and the new consumers are grateful to the government under
which this has happened. But material prosperity has had less
obvious results as well. As in the United States, the politics
of class are giving way to the politics of status. The British
are still a very class-conscious people, but they are less class-
conscious than they were. Young people especially are almost
as indifferent to class as their contemporaries in America. This
change has had a paradoxical result. The electors might have
been expected to turn to Labour as the traditional enemies of
class privilege. On the contrary, they have turned to the Conservatives—because Labour reminds them of a past they wish
to forget.

The Labour party was created to break through the walls
of privilege and give the workers a place in the sun. It was,
above all, a *class* party: even its name—"Labour" rather than
"Socialist"—is evidence of this. It drew its strength less from

an idea than from an almost instinctive response to the bitter memories of the industrial revolution. Its votes came from the gray cotton towns of the Northwest, the scarred industrial wilderness of the Black Country, the slag heaps of South Wales and Durham, the filthy slums of Glasgow, and the East End of London. Its earliest leaders—Keir Hardie, the miner; Ramsay MacDonald, the illegitimate son of a housemaid; Arthur Henderson, the iron smelter—were drawn from the authentic working class. Poverty had denied them any chance of education or advancement—and Labour politics was for them an opportunity for legitimate personal ambition, as well as for service to their fellows. From the beginning, Labour gave a hospitable welcome to middle-class allies, but the leaders for whom it reserved its warmth were working class, and proud of it. What has happened in the last ten years is that prosperity has started to wither the roots of a proletarian party. Technological change is killing the old industries and creating new occupations unsoured by the memory of old oppression. The filthy industrial slums are coming down at last; and their inhabitants are moving out to new housing estates in the suburbs. Above all, the educational ladder has been extended down to the bottom. Compared with the United States, the proportion of the population that goes to a university is still scandalously low, but it is high enough to cream off the ablest children of the working class. The Hardies, MacDonalds, and Hendersons of today are segregated from their less able playmates at the age of eleven, and they finish their education at twenty-two instead of at fifteen. The result of these changes is that the objective need for a primarily class-oriented progressive party has diminished—and at the same time its attractiveness has declined. Recent surveys show that for more and more people, Labour is the party of the underdog, the hopeless and helpless; the aged, the poor, the unskilled. But fewer and fewer people are willing to think of themselves as underdogs. For young people, especially, the Labour party is redolent of a forgotten past. . . .

There are . . . two reasons for believing that Labour may soon be forced to undergo a political facelift. The first is the Liberal revival. For years, the Liberal party was the coelacanth of British politics; extinct according to the textbooks, illogically alive in fact. In the past few years the Liberals have transformed themselves. Although they are in fact a very old party, they look very new. They are therefore perfectly situated to benefit from the social changes which have harmed Labour. The Liberals are progressive and lively; more responsive to the interests of the consumer than the other two parties; idealistic without being fanatical; egalitarian without being tied to any one class. The same surveys which show that the Labour party is seen as the party of the underdog show that the Liberals are seen as the party of the progressive-minded, the alert, the ambitious. If the Labour party remains set in its ways, the Liberal voters will eventually overtake it. When that happens, Labour voters will desert en masse. British voters have a healthy distaste for wasting their votes. For thirty years, Liberals have voted Labour to keep the Conservatives out. If the Liberals began to advance, would-be Labour voters would desert to the Liberals. This is still a distant prospect, but Labour's civil war has brought it nearer.

The struggle in the Labour party is, in fact, the strongest reason for believing that Labour will be forced to change. If the left wins, the right will for all practical purposes be forced out of the party—into alliance with the Liberals. If the Gaitskellites win, they will be strong enough to stamp their image on the party—and there will no longer be any need for a Liberal party. In either case, the end result is the same. There will be a small, extremist party opposed to NATO and advocating old-style nationalization; and a larger, more moderate, force, committed to NATO and with a more empirical social policy. The moderate party might be called either "Liberal" or "Labour," depending on circumstances. But the name does not matter. The important question is how long it takes to come into existence.

THE ECONOMY [4]

Britain lives by manufacture and trade. Its agriculture provides only half the food it needs and, apart from coal and low-grade iron ore, it has few natural resources. The other half of its food and most of the raw materials for its industries have to be imported and paid for mainly by exports of manufactures, and by its net earnings from overseas investment, shipping, tourism and a variety of commercial and financial services. Any remaining gap has to be filled by drawings on foreign currency reserves.

During the nineteenth century Britain secured a leading position in the world as manufacturer, merchant, carrier, banker and investor and so was able to support a rapidly increasing population (from about 12 million in 1801 to over 38 million in 1901) at a rising standard of living. In this period, it became largely dependent on imports which, by 1870, were 28 per cent of net national income at factor cost compared with only 12 per cent in 1820. (The present proportion is around 25 per cent.)

After the First World War, the world demand for the products of its staple industries—textiles, coal, heavy engineering—fell away, and Britain was slow at first in seeking compensation in the expanding world trade in the new engineering products such as cars and electrical goods. . . . Imports remained high, as the effect of a fall in the volume of exports was cushioned by favorable terms of trade and income from overseas investments. The slump in world trade was the largest factor in bringing about heavy unemployment which reached a peak of 22 per cent in 1932.

After 1932 production and employment increased following an increase in home investment, and some revival in world trade. A further stimulus to activity after 1935 was provided by the armament program.

Then came the Second World War and Britain's economy was fully employed in the war effort. Serious losses were incurred: domestic capital was run down—through shipping losses,

4 From *Britain in Brief*, pamphlet. British Information Services. 45 Rockefeller Plaza. New York 20. '59. p 11-15. Reprinted by permission.

bomb damage and arrears of industrial maintenance or replacement—by about £3,000 million; exports fell by 1944 to less than one third of the 1938 volume; the real value of the gold and dollar reserves was reduced to about half the prewar level; over £1,000 million of overseas investments were sold to pay for war supplies and other "invisible" earnings were suspended; and new external debts totaling £3,000 million were incurred.

These losses greatly increased the difficulty and the urgency of Britain's reconversion to a viable peacetime economy at the end of the war. A large increase in exports was required, especially as the rise in import prices had caused a deterioration in the terms of trade between 1938 and 1948.

Helped by loans and other aid from the United States and Canada—which paid for about one fifth of Britain's imports between 1946 and 1950—reconversion and recovery were rapid. Over the period 1946-1958, the average annual rate of increase in the real national product has been 3 per cent and in industrial production about 5 per cent. Until 1952 most of this increased output went into exports—which regained their prewar volume as early as 1947 and are now approximately double the 1938 volume; into investments to make good the destruction and run-down of capital during the war; and, after 1950, into rearmament. Since 1952, however, the individual consumer has benefited substantially from increased output. High production has been accompanied by a high level of employment, except in Northern Ireland where the unemployment rate has averaged some 8 per cent of the number of employees, while in Great Britain it has rarely exceeded 2 per cent.

In the early postwar years of shortage, a variety of controls over production, trade and consumption were in force. Most of these controls were removed by the end of 1954; and in 1958-1959 all but a very few of those remaining, which affected external trade and payments, were withdrawn.

Britain's main economic problem today is to increase still further its overseas earnings in order to pay for the imports needed by its expanding economy, to build up its reserves and to meet its commitments on account of debt, defense and development overseas within a climate of price stability at home. Its success depends on a continuing growth of world production and trade, and on its ability to secure a sufficient share of this trade which, in turn, depends upon the competitive strength of its goods in overseas markets. Its present share in world exports of manufactures is about 18 per cent compared with 22 per cent in 1937.

The National Income

If countries are grouped by national income per head of population (a very approximate measure of living standards) the United States and Canada are in the top group, while Britain is in the next group, together with Norway, Sweden, Denmark, Switzerland, Australia and New Zealand.

Britain's gross national product (national income plus depreciation) in 1958 was estimated at £20,114 million [£1= $2.80].

Manufacturing makes the greatest contribution (nearly two fifths) to the total home output of goods and services (gross domestic product). Agriculture, forestry and fishing together contribute a little under one twentieth; so does mining and quarrying; and building and contracting slightly more than one twentieth. About one fifth of Britain's total supplies are imported.

Of these supplies, rather over a half, on average, has been claimed in recent years by personal consumption and one fifth by exports. Investment has taken about one sixth and current expenditure by the central Government and local authorities about one seventh.

There has been a significant change in the distribution of personal income. Employees' incomes have risen from 60 per cent of total personal income in 1938 to 70 per cent in 1958, while income from self-employment has fallen from 13 to 10 per cent and income from rent, dividends and interest from 22 to 12 per cent. Over the period 1938-1958 the value of total wages and salaries in real terms has increased by over 60 per cent while that of dividends has decreased by nearly a quarter. Since

1948 dividends on share capital have taken about one quarter of company incomes compared with about one half in 1938.

Full employment, the increase and leveling up of employees' incomes and the redistributive effects of taxation have resulted in concentrating the bulk (about 70 per cent) of personal incomes after tax in the income range £250 to £1,000 [$700 to $2,800] a year. Compared with 1938, the share taken by the largest incomes has declined: in 1938, 8 per cent of total incomes after tax was taken by incomes of over £2,000 a year; in 1958, the percentage was less than 4.

About four fifths of personal income in 1958 was spent on consumption. Nearly one seventh went in taxes on income and in national insurance contributions, and about one sixth of consumers' expenditure was accounted for by indirect taxes.

In 1958, about 32 per cent of personal consumption went on food; 14 per cent on drink and tobacco; 14 per cent on housing, fuel and lighting; 9 per cent on clothing; 7 per cent on durable goods, cars and motor cycles; and 24 per cent on other goods and services.

Living Standards

The average level of food consumption is high (about 3,160 calories and 84 grains of protein per head daily). Consumption of fresh and frozen meat has risen to nearly 100 pounds per head per annum. About two families in three have television sets (there are 9.5 million licenses held) and vacuum cleaners, and one in three a washing machine, and one in seven a refrigerator. The number of private cars in use has doubled since 1950 and in 1958 exceeded 4.5 million.

SLOW ECONOMIC PROGRESS [5]

Britain was criticized today for letting her economy fall behind those of France and West Germany.

The criticism, following complaints voiced . . . at the Conservative party conference in Scarborough, came from the highly

[5] From "British Economy Reported Lagging," by W. H. Waggoner, New York *Times* correspondent. New York *Times*. p 23. O. 16, '60. Reprinted by permission.

respected, nonpartisan research organization, Political and Economic Planning.

In a pamphlet that will be the introduction of a larger study of Britain's economic growth . . . the organization warned that unless Britain gave priority to increasing her rate of growth, she would be outpaced by her Western European neighbors.

The study is further evidence of a new tendency here to scrutinize British economic activity.

At the Conservative party conference, Maurice Macmillan, son of the Prime Minister, asserted that to keep pace with the rate of German investment in industry Britain would have to put £500 million ($1,400 million) more a year into industry.

A week ago a Government report criticized the British shipbuilding industry for technical backwardness and failure to improve its productivity. The great advances by foreign shipyards were emphasized. An earlier report made similar criticisms of the British machine tool industry.

The Political and Economic Planning study says more positive influence should be exercised by Government agencies in directing the private sector of the economy. . . .

The report says Britain can learn from the United States. It mentions such examples as training programs for industrial managers, management techniques, and technological advances.

Investment Rate High

Britain shows up badly in nearly every index of economic and industrial growth cited by the study. The exception is the relatively high rate of investment per worker, which is explained by the comparatively slow growth of the population.

The report says the reason for the lower rate of economic growth in Britain must lie in the lower efficiency and productivity of the investment that has been made.

It notes that between 1950 and 1959, industrial production in Western Germany increased 125 per cent, and . . . in Britain 29 per cent.

"For some years it was possible to assume that the Germans were still making up for the loss of output in the 1940's," the pamphlet says. "But soon even the comparison with 1938 became unfavorable for the United Kingdom."

"More recent estimates have shown that after 1955 German industrial productivity went ahead rapidly each year," the report says. "British productivity showed little change, at least until 1959."

NUCLEAR ENERGY IN BRITAIN [6]

Work in Britain on nuclear energy, or energy released from the nucleus of the atom, has been going on since the beginning of the present century. Many of the early experiments which paved the way for its application to research and power production took place at the Cavendish Laboratory, Cambridge, where Rutherford accomplished the transmutation of nitrogen in 1919, Chadwick discovered the neutron, Cockcroft and Walton first split nuclei (of lithium) into alpha particles in 1932 and, a little later, fusion reactions were first observed.

Today Britain has some thirty-five reactors, either in operation or under construction, for research, testing and power production; has large factories producing fissile material in bulk; is the world's largest exporter of radioisotopes; has had operating, since May 1956, the world's first large-scale nuclear power station at Calder Hall, Cumberland; has embarked on an extensive ten-year nuclear program to develop 6,000 megawatts of electricity in this way by 1967; has available the industrial capacity to export complete nuclear power stations for use anywhere in the world; and, with research assemblies such as Zeta, Sceptre III and Maggi, has made notable progress towards the achievement of controlled thermonuclear reactions (the fusion process).

Organization

General responsibility for nuclear energy rests with the Prime Minister, to whom it was transferred from the Lord President of the Council in March 1957. Development activity, except the ordering of nuclear weapons (a function of the Minister of

[6] Fact sheet. (Fact Sheets on Britain R 2541/19) British Information Services. 45 Rockefeller Plaza. New York 20. '59. Reprinted by permission.

Supply) and the ordering of commercial nuclear power stations (for which the Minister of Power and the electricity authorities are responsible), is controlled by the United Kingdom Atomic Energy Authority (UKAEA), set up in 1954.

The establishments of the UKAEA are divided into three groups: the Industrial Group, with headquarters at Risley, Lancashire, controlling the so-called atomic factories and experimental nuclear power stations; the Research Group, responsible for nuclear research and the development and production of radioisotopes, with headquarters at Harwell, Berkshire, a second establishment at Winfrith Heath, Dorset, and a number of outstations, notably the Radiochemical Centre at Amersham; and the Weapons Group, with headquarters at Aldermaston, Berkshire, concerned with experimental work and the development and production of warheads for nuclear weapons as required by the Minister of Supply for defense purposes. [The latter was the terminus of the 1959 protest march described in "The Campaign for Nuclear Disarmament," in Section IV, below.]

A National Institute for Research in Nuclear Science was set up by the Government in March 1957, to provide facilities and equipment for common use by universities and others. One of the world's largest proton synchrotrons (particle accelerators) is being built for it at the Rutherford High Energy Laboratory, located at Harwell. An Admiralty committee is studying reactor systems for marine propulsion on an economic basis.

Reactors

Nuclear reactors (or atomic piles as they are sometimes called) are devices in which the splitting of heavy atoms of certain radioactive substances takes place slowly under controlled conditions, releasing a steady output of heat and a stream of neutrons, radiations and other particles. The smaller experimental reactors are valuable for their radiations rather than as heat sources. These radiations are used in research and also to create new artificial substances—mainly radioisotopes of naturally occurring substances.

Britain's experimental reactors are nearly all housed in the establishments of the UKAEA, though at least one private firm has built an experimental fission reactor (Merlin) and a fusion apparatus (Sceptre III). At Harwell there are at present working: Gleep (100 kilowatts, started in 1947); Bepo (6,000 kilowatts, started in 1948, the principal source of radioisotopes in Europe— the value of annual production at Harwell and Amersham is currently running at about £650,000 a year and exports go to over fifty countries); Zephyr (100 watts, experimental breeder reactor, producing more fissile material than it consumes, started in 1954); Dimple (a few watts, low-power enriched uranium heavy water reactor, started in 1954); Dido (10 megawatts, using almost pure U235 and heavy water as moderator, started in 1956, the most powerful reactor of its kind in Western Europe); Pluto (10 megawatts, similar to Dido, started in 1957); Zeus (100 watts, started in 1955—a breeder reactor to provide information for the Dounreay project, see below); Lido (100 kilowatts, a "swimming pool" reactor using ordinary water as moderator); Nero (a new experimental low energy reactor); Neptune (a zero energy reactor for studying problems of nuclear marine propulsion). Harwell also houses the largest isotope separator in Europe, Hermes, and the experimental apparatus Zeta (zero energy thermonuclear assembly).

Other experimental reactors of the UKAEA are housed at Calder Hall (two at Calder Hall A, and two at Calder Hall B— all working by the end of 1958), at Chapelcross, Annan, Dumfriesshire, Scotland (first reactor started at the end of 1958), and at Dounreay, Caithness, Scotland, which includes a breeder reactor due to operate in the spring of 1959 for experiment and for plutonium and electricity production. In 1958 Horace (a zero energy reactor) started operating at the Atomic Weapons Establishment, Aldermaston.

Nuclear Power Stations

Britain's energy requirements are expected to increase by about 20 per cent over the next decade, and the extensive development of nuclear power will reduce dependence upon additional imported supplies of oil, involving a heavy burden on the balance of payments.

In addition to the UKAEA reactors mentioned above, some of which produce electricity on a sizeable scale, the electricity authorities are planning to build up to 14 nuclear power stations by 1967, capable of producing about 6,000 megawatts of electricity [recently reduced to a capacity of 5,000 megawatts] and saving 18 million tons of coal or, alternatively, 10 million tons of oil. The total cost of this program over the decade will be about £900 million. The first four stations in this program are under construction by four of the five consortia of United Kingdom companies specially formed to build complete nuclear power stations. The stations will be at Bradwell in Essex, at Berkeley in Gloucestershire, at Hunterstone on the Ayrshire coast of Scotland, and at Hinkley Point, Somerset. Sites for further stations at Trawsfynnyd, North Wales, at Dungeness, Kent, at Sizewell, Suffolk, and in Northern Ireland, are being considered.

A United Kingdom consortium received the world's first export order for a nuclear power station—one of the Calder Hall type, of 200 megawatts—for an Italian electricity supply organization. A United Kingdom firm has a share in an order for a 22 megawatt nuclear power station in Cuba. Other contracts are under negotiation.

Safety and Health

Precautions taken in nuclear energy establishments in the United Kingdom ensure that the risk to workers' health is less than that in many other industries. Great care is also taken to ensure the safe disposal of radioactive wastes, some of which, such as strontium 90 and caesium 137, are put to useful work in electricity and medicine. The United Kingdom Medical Research Council has had committees studying the effect of radiation for ten years, and, in June 1956, one such committee, appointed in 1955 at the request of the Government, published a report which showed, among other things, that the radiation received by the population of Britain from UKAEA's projects was only about 0.1 per cent of that received from natural sources, such as cosmic rays. The UKAEA has a Health Advisory Committee, a Safety Executive Committee, a Reactor Safety Committee, and an Ancillary Establishments Supply Committee. In 1958, a new Advisory Committee on Training in Radiological Protection was formed.

Training

Universities and technical colleges, as well as the UKAEA, all help in training the scientists and technologists needed for nuclear development in Britain and the Commonwealth and throughout the world. The research establishment at Harwell runs both isotope and reactor schools, a considerable proportion of whose students come from overseas. Arrangements have been made to train overseas technicians and scientists to operate the research reactors in process of being established in several countries. There is also a reactor operations school at Calder Hall.

TOWN PLANNING IN LONDON [7]

London is being methodically rebuilt to a massive master plan, the first stage of which is to be completed . . . [in 1960], the second stage in 1975, and the final stage in 2005. Nothing so comprehensive has been attempted since the great fire of 1666, when the inspired London of Christopher Wren was born.

The Londoner himself, traveling his well-worn line from home to office and home again, knows less of it than the visitor. There is the 351-foot Shell Oil tower, which is mounting cacophonously day by day to dominate the Thames's south bank. Across the river at Millbank, behind Big Ben, rises the beginning of the 387-foot Vickers block, the first London building taller than St. Paul's. But one really needs to explore beyond, from Peckham Rye to the Seven Sisters Road, to glimpse the scope of the great plan that rolls on toward the next century.

[7] From "Atlantic Report on the World Today—London." *Atlantic Monthly.* 205:26+. Je. '60. Reprinted by permission.

This plan was initiated by Lord Reith in 1941, and it still visibly bears the stamp of this purposeful Scot who earlier developed the earnest, noncommercial, and sometimes brilliant British Broadcasting Corporation. The architect of the New London Plan was the eminent professor, Sir Patrick Abercrombie. The plan is under the supervision of the London County Council, administrator of the 117 square miles of the County of London. The L.C.C. has been Socialist-controlled for twenty-five years and is experienced in planning.

Its first aim is to stop London's family from growing. The second is to move tens of thousands in overpopulated fringe areas out of the town altogether. The third is to bring into the center a quite new resident population. The fourth is to build a final city of interconnected twentieth-century country towns, in brick and concrete, each complete in itself and set in park land.

New Space for Living

At night now, the city abruptly empties and is left to visitors and janitors. The plan is to change it back to what it was, a home as well as a hotel and a workshop. The first step toward this goal is the erection of the Barbican, a community for fifty thousand on a site now being prepared out of the rubble of tumble-down warehouses in the original City. The Barbican is to be a city within the City, with traffic-free squares and terraces laid out between triangular tower apartments, its own stores, schools, art center, swimming pool, roof gardens, hotels, and restaurants. Homes for another five thousand new Londoners are to be built nearby at Finsbury. In the West End, the first new private-enterprise apartment block is going up in the Charing Cross Road.

The L.C.C. meanwhile is trying hard to control the flood tide of office building. Since 1955, all applications to turn theaters into offices have been refused. Seventy large firms have been persuaded to move their main offices out of central London. Almost all industry, except immovable heavy industries along the banks of London's river, is to be served with notices to vacate. The L.C.C. is spending $1.5 million a year to buy out those industries that own the land they stand on. The small workshops which are traditional, as in the East End, are to be housed tier on tier in tall buildings.

To gain more space for living, 20,000 Londoners are being moved out of town each year. There are 150,000 cockneys on new estates in the suburbs, 50,000 in new satellite towns, and 30,000 settled already in existing country towns.

The three million who are to stay in the county will live more spaciously in three hundred "neighborhoods," neat apartment villages lying off the main roads and linked in groups of five to sixty "communities." Each community is to have its own senior high schools, big stores, art and technical colleges, and town halls. The aim is to provide at least four acres of park and playground per thousand people and to strive for seven acres.

A good place to get the feel of the London that is planned for 2005 is a hill in Richmond Park. From there the powerful rectangles of the regular white towers of Roehampton stand guard at intervals over a low, crowded, higgledy-piggledy London, the town of the past. The effect of discipline is softened by grass and trees, and the view has beauty.

The Traffic Problem

The great plan, as it stands now, faces one unforeseen enemy —the automobile. "Building more roads to be filled with more cars is not the solution, as the Americans have found." Armed with this conviction and charged by law "to preserve the best of existing London and respect its structure," as well as build anew, the L.C.C. fights a rear-guard action to keep its New London Plan intact. But without more roads, and perhaps even without a quite differently conceived city, how can the equation be solved? Hundreds of thousands of newly made commuters, moved by the L.C.C. itself from the fringes to suburbs and satellites, plus tens of thousands of new resi-

dents attracted into the very center, with their cars—what is
the answer?

Into this controversy has been thrust a new political figure—
Ernest Marples, eager, effervescent, efficient, and eccentric, and
a self-made man. . . . Above all, Mr. Marples is a construction man. He has, by British political custom, disposed of his
holdings in Marples, Ridgeway Limited, now that he is Minister
of Transport. His name, however, stays on the bulldozers and
giant shovels at Hammersmith Broadway, where London's second overpass is being built on the road to London Airport. . . .

Mr. Marples' first act has been to frame a bill making
himself virtual traffic dictator of London. His authority super-
sedes the established powers hitherto exercised by the L.C.C.,
the twenty-eight boroughs of the county, and almost eighty
other local authorities and committees in the Greater London
that reaches out beyond the county boundary.

With this authority Mr. Marples plans to tear up traffic
islands in the middle of bridges and main roads, introduce
a free flow of traffic at rush hours, mark plainly in white
paint where motorists can park in London and where they
cannot, recruit traffic wardens to free Scotland Yard from the
tedious duties that now take up more than half its policemen's
time, scatter the town with parking meters, and put car parks
underneath the trees and lawns of Hyde Park. He is in constant
touch with Baltimore, which he considers provides America's
finest example of traffic engineering, to keep this five-year plan
up to date. He is working on a ten-year plan to follow. And
he has set up a long-term study group to "produce a 'design
for living' at the turn of the century."

The car seems likely to bring even more profound changes
to Britain. For it provides a special challenge to an island
so crowded, so settled, and so old. Already there is an automobile for every one and a half yards of main road; there are
forty-five cars to every mile of road, lane, and by-way. By
1975, the year of the end of stage two of the New London Plan,
there will, at the present rate, be just eighteen inches of main
traffic highway to each car.

The Auto Industry

Many economists, as well as many planners, are beginning to warn that the automobile industry is expanding too fast. It was a shock to some of them when the budget produced no extra tax to slow the industry down, even though a new car already bears a 50 per cent sales tax. But demand is still so urgent in spite of the tax that the British industry plans to increase output by 70 per cent in three years to meet it. By 1962 production will probably be three million vehicles, three times as many as 1952.

THE AFFLUENT SOCIETY IN BRITAIN [8]

The Affluent Society is under attack. Geologists doubt whether there are enough natural resources in the earth's crust to go on supporting it, sociologists are baffled because it has upset traditional theories about the relation between poverty and crime, Socialists deplore it because voters prefer it to socialism, and even Conservatives mistrust it and are slightly ashamed of having won a general election on a slogan which implied that most people were better off than ever before. Having struggled for two centuries to cure the poverty and misery which were the by-products of the industrial revolution, we seem at a loss now that we are in sight of our goal.

But first, how affluent are we? Statistics paint a confused picture. Last year the average earnings of the British working man were just over £14 [about $39] a week, high but still a good deal lower than the earnings of many Negro workers in the southern United States. But average earnings do not give one much idea of the character of a community. They include millions of family men who earn £10 [$28] a week or less, and about two million who earn £20 [$56] a week or more.

There are men working at the coal-face in modern collieries, drawers in brickyards, crane drivers, stereotype operators and

[8] From "Our Affluent Society," by Aidan Crawley, formerly a member of Parliament and currently a writer of TV documentaries. *Sunday Times* (London). p 10. O. 2, '60. Reprinted by permission.

some machine operators who earn between £25 [$70] and £50 [$140] a week. But although these manual workers get more than many people in offices they work much harder, often getting up regularly at 5 A.M., sometimes working six and even seven days a week. There are not yet many wage-earners with both high incomes and lots of leisure, the twin attributes of affluence.

Too Good to Last?

And yet the picture is still not complete. Many wage-earners have sons, daughters or wives living in their homes who are also bringing in a wage-packet; usually it is the family income that matters. Perhaps a better guide to the way we live lies in the sums spent at Christmas and on holidays, the volume of the hire-purchase [installment-payment] debt, the amount spent by teenagers on clothes and gramophone records. In the aggregate these sums are vast; the hire-purchase debt alone works out at nearly £50 [$140] a head of the working population, and expenditure at Christmas and on holidays has been steadily rising.

Teenage spending has earned a place in our national records. Apart from what they give their parents it amounts to about £4 [about $11] a head per week. It is plain therefore that in many households, where there is more than one wage-earner, anything from £200 [$560] to £500 [$1400] a year is being spent on things which cannot be classed as necessities.

One might compare our society to a sow's litter. Of the ten little pigs, one is weak, never getting quite enough food and having to be assisted. Eight are doing well, jostling each other for all they can get. One, bigger than the rest, always gets the best place and looks fattest and sleekest.

We still have a submerged tenth, people who are poor and have to be assisted. We still have a top tenth, rich and getting richer. And the great majority of us are doing steadily better, spending more each year on leisure and pleasure, [and] if not affluent, beginning to taste what affluence means.

Yet, if we are honest with ourselves, all of us live in fear that it is too good to last.

The reason, I believe, is psychological. We still cannot shake off the past. Our political and economic thinking is a hangover from the years of struggle when uncertainty, unemployment and poverty were the main facts of life.

Conquest of Poverty

I am not suggesting that poverty has vanished from Britain. Last year 2,346,000 people claimed National Assistance, and although 349,000 were refused it, it does not follow that many of them were not destitute; for the reasons for refusal are often technical and due to an over-rigid interpretation of National Assistance rules.

There are still nearly 2 million applicants for houses on council lists. The overcrowding in our slums is as bad, though not as general, as in Moscow; and slum clearance is behind schedule. At a guess therefore, in a population of 50 million, there must be between 4 and 5 million men, women and children who at best find life hard and at worst live in misery.

But in spite of these facts—and they are formidable—the most significant thing about poverty in Britain is that it is no longer generally noticeable. It is both localized and scattered. There are areas, like Clydeside [the Glasgow shipbuilding area on the Firth of Clyde] and Merseyside [the industrial, commercial, and trading area centering about Liverpool], where unemployment is heavy and you can *see* it, in the queues at the labor exchanges and in the faces of the people. But how many of us in the greater part of these islands know people who buy none but secondhand clothes? Or see children (and there are more children in London than before the war) who are undernourished?

The truth is that for all its extent, poverty is no longer a disease of the country as a whole. Poverty is still a challenge, but it is no longer *the* problem of our time.

Nor, in the political field, is equality. For generations equality has been the mainspring of democratic political life. And, of course, when most people had far too little and a few far too much, equality *was* a goal. No one then needed to ask "equality with what?" As soon as a certain degree of equality has been reached, however, as it has today, it either ceases to be a goal or it demands constant change.

But once people have enough to be comfortable most of them do not want change. When coalminers are told they ought to be thankful that pits are being closed so that they can at last enjoy the amenities of work above ground, they are angry and resentful. They do not wish to be equal with those who work above ground, they wish to remain miners. . . .

Even equality of opportunity has lost its drive as a slogan. It implies a great unsatisfied urge to grasp opportunity. But opportunity involves the acceptance of responsibility, and the truth, as we are now beginning to discover, is that the number of those who welcome responsibility is very small. Men who have been used to taking orders dislike being criticized and giving up fixed hours of work. They want, not opportunity, but security.

Equality of education is not only an absurdity but a contradiction. I am not suggesting that we should not provide everyone with the best possible education, but it is the inequalities in men that education develops, and that constitute the richness of society.

Turning the Signposts

If we are to understand affluence and make the most of it, almost all our social and political signposts need turning round the other way. For affluence does not mean the end of our problems but rather that our problems are the opposite of those to which we have been accustomed.

For example, our chief concern today is not unemployment but full employment. Today on Clydeside there may be three men for every advertised job, but there are six vacancies for every man applying in the Midlands, and in London and other parts of the South as many as eighteen vacancies. And important though it is to see that men in Glasgow get work it is even more important for the community to see that vacancies in the rest of the country are filled. In the long run this is the cure for Glasgow too.

The present generation of politicians and planners was brought up on mass unemployment, low wages and fluctuating demand. Today they are faced with a shortage of men, particularly men with managerial and technical skills, with hidden overstaffing because employers are afraid to let men go, and with high and stable demand.

We know comparatively little about these new problems. None of the Government retraining schemes have succeeded in attracting enough men to provide the new skills; after twenty years of full employment we are still short of good managers, scientists, technologists, draftsmen. Since we are also desperately short of trained teachers, it is doubtful if our traditional program of education will supply the deficiencies. We still allow experienced men to retire in their prime. Ours being a small country, it ought to be easy for people to travel to new centers of work from their homes; but we have spent so little on roads or on the approaches to our cities that even this advantage is thrown away.

It is not just a question of priority or even of urgency, it is a great psychological change that is needed. Harsh though it may sound, we must break our obsession with the underdog and devote our attention to the dogs that are on the way up.

Our social insurance is an excellent example of what I mean. It was designed to "set a bottom to poverty," and perhaps a tenth of the population still need that bottom. Nine tenths still need insurance, but for quite other things.

When men become redundant today they normally find other jobs quite quickly. This does not mean that they do not suffer anxiety or expense. They may have farther to go to the new job, perhaps to accept a lower wage. If they have to move their homes—and nearly half a million people have changed the region in which they work in each of the last two years—their expenses are enormously increased. These liabilities of full employment should be included in our general social insurance.

Even danger signals like "inflation" need looking at anew. It is heresy today to question the terrors of inflation. Chancellors of the Exchequer are haunted by it, and in his pamphlet "Labour and the Affluent Society" Mr. [Anthony] Crossman calls it "the curse of Western capitalism." But over the past three decades it has been proved that the deliberate extension or contraction of credit is the proper regulator of a free economy, and in fact the control has been brilliantly used. What we need is confidence in it.

Inflation is not a bogy but a tool. Full employment may lead to inflation; but controlled inflation is also the means by which full employment is secured. When a Chancellor alters the conditions of hire purchase, changes the bank rate or puts pressure on banks to restrict overdrafts, we ought to wake up in the morning feeling that the world is a saner, securer place.

Appetites and Needs

It is only when we shake off our memories and look at the world as it is that we can give some shape to the affluent society. For the future of affluence is concerned not only with traditional problems but with tastes and appetites—things about which as a country we have hardly begun to think at all.

The difficulty is that, once appetites have ceased to be *needs,* they lie dormant and need stimulating; and at the moment the process of stimulation is mainly in the hands of the advertiser. And in the main the advertiser represents the manufacturer. Just when we are reaching a suggestible stage, able to relax and make a choice, we are subjected to an intensive bombardment aimed at inducing us to buy an endless succession of refinements of the things with which we are already familiar.

In Britain at the moment this may be no great danger, since production has not lost touch with real needs and there is plenty of room for improvement. But there are warning signs. If every detergent washes "whiter," does it matter much which we buy? Do we really need to work hard to produce a gadget for switching from one television channel to another without getting out of our chair?

Obviously there is a point at which we should stop and ask ourselves whether what we are producing is really worth while. Already most of us like to boast that we work hard, when our aim is to work just hard enough. Is the instinct to take things easy stupid or uncivilized? Now that we can comfortably produce all our basic needs, is greater productivity the only goal?

The standard answer is that we live by trade and must strive continually to beat our competitors. Up to a point this is true. But a nation can thrive and be cultured without having the highest income per head in the world.

A Distorted Reflection

Our problem therefore is not simply one of productivity; it is increasingly one of selection. And the difficulty is to select without being stampeded either by the advertiser on the one hand or the Socialist on the other. Socialists will tell us what is good for us and deny us what is not. But to surrender our right of choice just when it becomes tantalizing is to throw away all that we have struggled for.

The answer lies partly in education, towards which our attitude is not only traditional but parochial, partly in overhauling our whole conception of a "standard of living." Our "standard" has for generations been expressed only in goods and services individually paid for. So long as so much was lacking, this no doubt reflected what people hoped for from life. Today the reflection is distorted.

When nearly every other family has a motor car or motor bicycle the demand for better roads may be far stronger than for anything an individual may buy, but we have no means of assessing it. We do not pay to climb mountains or go hiking; we pay little to see pictures, read books, listen to music or spend a day by the sea. Yet, as we become affluent, more and more of us do these things.

Indeed we want far more information about how people live when they are *not* spending, about tastes which spring from leisure rather than need. In modern techniques of mass communication we have the means of discovering the likes and dislikes, habits and hopes of our society. If we have the imagination to use them we can set standards which will bring increasing affluence without involving us in a spiral of wasteful effort, or in the "race" to material prosperity which Socialists like Mr. Crossman so desperately want to win.

ARE THE ENGLISH BEING AMERICANIZED? [9]

There have been signs in the . . . [recent past] that London is rapidly losing some of its Englishness, and is becoming, as Englishmen describe it, Americanized.

What the word means is never easy to disentangle from the prejudice and misconceptions which surround it. But there seems little doubt that the resistance that London has already maintained against the importation of American ideas has become noticeably weaker. In the past, London—perhaps more than any other Western European capital—has proudly rejected the conveniences or simplifications of life that are roughly classified as "American."

Behind the superficial signs there have always been deep-rooted suspicions about American ways of life; the belief has been cherished that old Rolls Royces are better than brand-new Cadillacs, and that cars, clothes, houses, or radios should be built to last forever; that the family grocer is preferable to the supermarket, and that fallible small firms are better than infallible big ones. Much of this attitude is, of course, no more than innate British conservatism, which gives way slowly to any kind of new idea; it is a conservatism that is exemplified at its best in the London taxi, which is old-fashioned, sedate, but very comfortable—and at its worst in British plumbing. Underlying the conservatism is not only the dislike of change, but also the

[9] From article by Anthony Sampson, British author and journalist. *Saturday Review.* 42:14-15. O. 17, '59. Reprinted by permission.

conviction that there are traditions and rules which are more important than money or efficiency.

To many Englishmen, watching Italy, Germany, and France changing their faces in the early years after the war, with glass palaces, Chevrolets, and chewing gum, it had seemed for a time as though Great Britain might be inured against the influences of America. With the help of a dollar shortage and strict control of construction, outwardly London has managed to preserve an astonishing old-fashionedness.

But now, with the boom, the end of the credit squeeze, and the biggest building program since 1939, Britain is quickly changing. The skyline is only the visual evidence; much more important is the way the whole character of British business and trade seems to be turning.

The family grocers, who take five minutes to find the marmalade, are being gravely threatened by the new supermarkets, whose success in Britain has been even more spectacular than in the States—if only because the old shops have been less competent. Precooked and frozen foods have swept the country: broiled chickens on spits, unheard of three years ago, are now revolving in nearly every high-street. Late-night shopping, quick-serving restaurants, hamburger bars (discreetly renamed "Wimpy bars"), and self-service cafes have sprouted up between the sleepy grocers and the dainty tea shops.

More fundamental, the whole pattern of buying is beginning to change. The old British idea of goods "made to last a lifetime" is disappearing. *Very* old cars are still fashionable, but the practice of buying a new one every three years is spreading quickly. The price of secondhand automobiles is falling accordingly, while new models are taking on the glittering, chromium-plated look of their American counterparts. Radios, refrigerators, gramophones, even ladies' apparel, are exhibiting the same tendency towards rapid replacement: the head of one of the biggest women's clothing shops remarked the other day that he could no longer sell coats that would be durable for decades. His coats are now tailored to last but two seasons.

While British consumers are beginning to mimic the American pattern of constant replenishment, large British firms have been undergoing their own radical transformations. In the past six months there has been an unprecedented number of "raids"—or "takeover bids," in the English phrase (an expression that was itself scarcely known by the British public two years ago). . . .

The most controversial of these bids was the great "Aluminium War" of . . . January [1959], when Reynolds Metals of America, acting through British Tube Investments, purchased the only English aluminum firm, after an unprecedented and bitter tussle, which ended in a consortium of British banks allying themselves unsuccessfully to stop the deal. The battle between the American company and the conservative forces of the City [the London financial center] generally regarded as the stronghold of "The Establishment" (the supposed aristocratic ruling class of Britain, centering round the Queen), showed in dramatic form the changing shape of Britain. The City bankers believed, as the wags put it, that they "were saving British Aluminium for civilization." The fact that The Establishment lost—even though the City was not united in the alliance—has not been forgotten.

Since the Aluminium War, there has been a succession of takeovers, not usually directly involving American businesses but embracing American methods. Two of the most spectacular . . . [of these represent] a dramatic clash between strong, new business techniques and the orthodox ideas of The Establishment.

The first has been the bid by a tough Scots shopkeeper, Hugh Fraser, for Harrods, the largest and grandest department store in Britain. Patronized by the Queen herself, Harrods has cherished a long and venerable tradition, ignoring many of the rules of costing and time-and-motion study. With its acres of grand pianos, its courteous shop assistants, and its patience in waiting for payment of accounts, it has epitomized the Victorian idea of "dignity in commerce." Fraser, bent on becoming Britain's master-shopkeeper, offered the astonishing figure of £37 million [$103.6 million] for Harrods and its associates—a sum that can only be explained by his desire to exploit its prestige. It is almost like buying part of Buckingham Palace.

The second instance has been the purchase by the Canadian press magnate, Roy Thomson, of the Kemsley group of newspapers, which includes the highly respected and successful *Sunday Times,* whose front page bears the royal coat of arms. Thomson, who has built his fortune with a chain of small-town Canadian newspapers, and latterly with television in Scotland, has evidently, like Fraser, determined to buy prestige: the *Sunday Times* is not so august as Harrods and not so grand as its daily namesake, the *Times;* but it has some of the mystique attached to a conservative and unchanging newspaper.

Thomson and Fraser bring to their properties all the harsh realism of single-minded business methods, together with the knowledge, that prestige, like any other commodity, is marketable. While these two changes cannot be charged to America, there is a general impression that they reflect the American way of doing things.

The success of the new British tycoons—Charles Clore, Isaac Wolfson, or Cecil King of the *Daily Mirror*—presents a difficult dilemma to the younger critics of Britain, sometimes loosely known as the "Angry Young Men," for up until now they have spent much of their time attacking The Establishment. Lord Portal, the ousted chairman of British Aluminium, was a figure in The Establishment; so was Lord Kemsley, the chairman of the *Sunday Times;* so, to a lesser extent, was Sir Richard Burbidge, chairman of Harrods. Thus, while the Young Angries are still training their guns on the environs of Buckingham Palace, they are discovering that many of these ancient institutions are no longer occupied by sedate and stuffy old Englishmen, but have been taken over by something more mysterious and perhaps more alarming: the cohorts of international big business.

The dilemma is not a superficial one, and it is echoed right through British social life. For some time now it has become clear that the British class system, which forms the ultimate protection against change, is beginning, however slowly, to dissolve. Most people, particularly the Young Angries and the

Socialists, will doubtless be glad to see it go. What perhaps its critics have not fully realized is that if one form of hierarchy is broken down, another is bound to take its place. If the old Etonians, the press barons, and the banking families are to disappear, they will be succeeded by those who are most ambitious and singleminded in the art of building personal and economic power. It is the class system—more than insularity, prejudice, or lethargy—which has undergirded British traditionalism; as it disintegrates, so an economic power hierarchy is bound to take its place, and not even a Socialist government can prevent it.

It would be rash to carry the generalization too far. Ever since Elizabethan times London has had a way of deflecting men's ambitions from pure profitmaking. Roy Thomson and Hugh Fraser may end up as peers, as their predecessors did; the grand pianos may remain in Harrods, and the *Sunday Times* may continue to serialize royal memoirs. Those in Britain who complain vaguely of "Americanization" should realize that, at the same time, the United States has in some respects also become more European. The two no longer represent opposite poles. Yet it remains true that a great deal of Britain is crumbling before our eyes; and we may be forgiven if—in spite of the boom and the new freedom and ease of our life—we shed a few tears.

ENGLAND AND HER RACE PROBLEM [10]

There are now more than fifty thousand West Indians in Britain, and several hundreds more come to join them every month. Early in 1955, the tabloid *Daily Sketch* ran a series of articles on "the Paradise Invasion" by "zoot-suited dupes" who are "doomed to poverty relieved only by the public purse." But to Fred Johnson, from Kingston, Jamaica, Britain is where there is work. We stood talking at a street corner in shabby Brixton, a decaying London borough which has come to serve as a kind of transit camp in which friends and relatives already there find room for immigrants while they look for jobs and

    [10] From "England Gets a Race Problem," by Norman MacKenzie, staff member of *New Statesman*. *Harper's Magazine*. 213:61-5. N. '56. Reprinted by permission.

homes of their own. Across the street, in a fine drizzle, a Salvation Army band was striking echoes from a brick wall on which, in four-foot letters, was painted the slogan KBW—"Keep Britain White."

"That don't worry we," Fred Johnson said. "Those fascists are crazy people. They aren't British like we." For Fred, like most of his fellow Jamaicans, is intensely patriotic. He is sensitive about his color, quick to feel discrimination, nostalgic for the warmth and vitality of his home island. But he also feels that he is British, and given a chance to settle in to British habits and conditions, he can belong.

For one thing, there is now nowhere else to go. Some West Indians I have talked to are wistful about the United States. They like to read Negro magazines such as *Ebony* and *Our World,* use Americanisms in their speech, and try to strike up friendships with Negro GI's from the air bases in Britain. There are, after all, nearly 300,000 British West Indians in the United States, and until recently the stream of migrants moved, not to Britain, but to Panama, Cuba, and the States. Emigration to Britain really began in 1948, and it is only . . . [since 1953] that special boats and charter flights have brought West Indians across the Atlantic in large numbers.

By United States standards, the numbers are still small. Only one person out of every thousand in the population is a West Indian. And only one immigrant comes from the West Indies for every seven from other parts of the Commonwealth. Nothing, one would say, to get excited about. The influx is tiny by comparison to the stream of Puerto Ricans arriving in New York, or to Negro migration into Chicago, Detroit, or San Francisco. Yet the West Indians are creating a new social problem for Britain. For the first time, Britain is having to face up to the question of color, not in the colonies, but in the streets, factories, dance halls and public houses of London, Birmingham, Leeds, and other industrial cities. And though West Indians are no more than half the colored minority in Britain, they are the center of the problem.

There are, I think, several reasons for this. First, they are much more visible, and they are more concentrated in certain areas. Secondly, they are not students, or seamen, or—like many Sikhs and Pakistanis—transients who have come to make some money to set themselves up at home. Most of the West Indians have come to settle in Britain, and they expect to be assimilated. Thirdly, they have no national or cultural tradition which sets them apart: the history, literature, and social patterns of Britain are accepted as much in Kingston, Jamaica, as in Kingston in Yorkshire. And, to the Englishman, this "similarity" is much harder to get along with than the differences he normally expects to find in a "foreigner." When a West Indian enters a factory, his work mates are often genuinely surprised to find that he speaks no other language than English and that he takes quite literally the entry on his passport which reads "British Subject by Birth."

For this passport is the legal token of equality. The law in Britain recognizes no differences of pigment. That is why many liberals hesitate even to discuss legislation or administrative action against discrimination—a fair employment code such as the FEPC, for example. If laws in *favor* of colored citizens can be passed, then a precedent is created, and there can equally well be laws *against* them. Such matters as the refusal to serve a colored man in a bar (licensing laws), or racialist comments in a dance hall (laws on insulting behavior), or even overcharging for rooms (redress is possible under the rent laws), are in any case equally actionable by white and West Indian. The law knows no color bar, and Mr. Osborne, a Conservative member of Parliament, made little headway with a bill designed to "regulate" immigration by "undesirables."

But law is different from custom. I have often heard a West Indian say that "there isn't a color bar, but . . ." and then add that it might be easier to know how things stood if there were a more distinct color line. Fred Johnson put this point well. "We can never be sure," he said. Never sure, that is, when someone will draw the line, and never sure whether what seems to be discrimination really is color prejudice. Many West Indians come to Britain believing that they are skilled workers—carpenters, for instance, or bricklayers, or electricians—and when they find skilled jobs closed to them they feel that it is too much color rather than too little skill that has lost them an opening. Yet employers and unions alike have found from experience that what passes for skill in Jamaica often doesn't come up to British standards. The difficulty is to persuade the West Indian that the employer is not simply finding an excuse.

Why Do They Come?

The ignorance of most British people about the West Indies is matched by West Indian ignorance about conditions in Britain. Traveling up from Dover with a trainload of immigrants I found that they had little conception of distance. One asked me how much a taxi would cost from the London terminus to an address in Birmingham—more than a hundred miles by road. When another told me he expected to stay with friends in Brixton, I was astonished when he announced that he did not know where they lived.

"I'll just stop the first colored man I see and ask him," he told me.

Others, arriving in unusually good summer weather, still found it chilly.

"I'm glad I got a strong suit," one said, showing me a light tweed jacket. "I'll be okay till it gets warmer."

There is so much to learn in a new country, not least the urban disciplines that are taken for granted by an Englishman and are unknown to most West Indians. And yet, even if they knew the difficulties that lay ahead, most of these immigrants would still come. Entry to Britain is unrestricted; it is simply a matter of raising the passage money by saving, selling tools or households goods, borrowing from money lenders or from relatives in Britain. And in Britain, there is both work and welfare. For the labor shortage is acute, while full employment lasts; and everyone is entitled to free medical treatment, to unemployment and sickness benefit, to pensions, and, in case of need, to National Assistance (relief). A West Indian may not succeed in getting the job he wants, at least for a beginning, and he may not earn at first as much as he expects (he usually knows that wages are higher in Britain than in Jamaica, but does not realize that prices are higher too). Yet a job can be found for him. And that is a sharp contrast with conditions at home. Income per head in Britain is $646, in Jamaica it is $170. This explains the migration.

Jamaicans are used to migration. But today, more than ever, it offers the only hope of escaping from stagnation at home. There one worker in five is unemployed. Thousands of young people have never worked at all. Yet, in the next ten years, the labor force will grow by one fifth: even if 210,000 new jobs could be created in the next decade (at the moment there are about half a million workers in industry, trade, and agriculture), unemployment would still be about 5 per cent. And there is no prospect of creating so many jobs. [There has been considerable progress in the West Indies since this article was written (1956) but not enough to solve the unemployment problem.—Ed.]. . .

Jamaica does not have sufficient resources to build industry, nor capital enough to modernize its agriculture. Britain could, and should, give more help than is offered at present, but no one sees much hope of ending chronic unemployment in the island or of creating a viable economy. There are simply too many people: in Jamaica, 1,400,000 live in 4,400 square miles; and in Barbados, pressure is even greater, 220,000 living in 166 square miles.

None of this needs stressing, any more than one need describe in detail the appalling housing conditions—four out of five dwellings in Kingston are one room, measuring ten by fifteen feet or less—or the social conditions, poor educational facilities, and outright beggary. The causes of migration from the British islands in the Caribbean are basically similar to those which drive Puerto Ricans to New York.

Yet many people in Britain were genuinely surprised when Mr. Norman Manley, the newly elected Chief Minister of Jamaica, selected an American to make an inquiry into West Indian migration to the British Isles. When in May 1955 he appointed Dr. Clarence Senior, Chief of the Migration Division of the Puerto Rican Department of Labor and an internationally respected expert, some newspapers asked why the task had not been given to a British sociologist, familiar with British conditions.

Norman Manley was right, however, and even the skeptics in Britain acknowledged this by the time that the go-getting Dr. Senior had finished his investigations. For he not only knew, from experience in New York and Puerto Rico, what patterns to look for, but he was also free from the unconscious and inhibiting assumptions that any social scientist is bound to make when he meets a color problem in his own country for the first time. Norman Manley could not afford to wait while painstaking academics piled up case studies; he needed his basic facts quickly.

When Clarence Senior left London in September 1955, he carried with him a briefcase containing twenty pounds of notes. By the end of the year, they had been translated into an official report from which, after careful examination, I can find no omission of any importance. With his assistant, Mr. Douglas Manley, the son of the Chief Minister, Dr. Senior conducted some hundreds of interviews, visited social clubs, factories, and all the neighborhoods to which West Indians have gone. In six weeks, he saw the problem whole. And, what is more important, his survey helped educate many people in Britain about this problem.

Before the Senior inquiry began, few people in Britain had realized that the arrival of thousands of West Indians was more than a somewhat accidental migration. Even those who knew that there was already a problem in certain areas had thought little further than measures to deal with those who had arrived. I was doing my own research at the same time as Dr. Clarence Senior, and I found only two or three experts who had realized that the 25,000 West Indians who . . . arrived in Britain in . . . [1953 and 1954 were] merely an advance guard. . . .

It's Not Me, It's Him

Apart from the handful of former fascists—Oswald Mosley's last hangers-on—no one in Britain openly insists that Britain should be kept white. There is, however, a strong but elusive undercurrent of prejudice, which crops up in unlikely places. One liberal intellectual, for instance, argued in this way for some restriction on colored immigration.

"We have no color problem in Britain," he said to me, "and therefore we have no color bar. But if the numbers of colored people increase, then we shall have a color bar. This would create new complications for us, for it would not only corrode our democracy from within, but it would also cause much embarrassment to visitors from the Commonwealth and Asia."

This person genuinely believed, from the most insular motives, that immigration restrictions would in the long run help maintain reasonable relations between the British and colored peoples. What he completely overlooked was the disastrous moral and political impact that such restrictions would make on Britain's claim to believe in democracy and racial justice.

A shop steward—a rank-and-file union leader—in one of Britain's auto factories at Coventry also disclaimed prejudice, but asked why, since British people could not emigrate freely to other parts of the Commonwealth, West Indians should be permitted to enter Britain as they pleased. By singling out the colored group, he distorted the picture. In fact, more people have left Brtiain since the war ended than have come as immigrants. Every year, there is a net loss of at least sixty thousand.

The unions, indeed, are one of the really difficult aspects of this problem. In September 1955, the Trades Union Congress passed a resolution affirming that its eight million affiliated members believed in racial equality and opposed any form of discrimination. Yet in March 1954, the Barbados Minister of Labour, Mr. Mapp, had declared that "the main opposition to the employment of West Indian workers comes from the rank and file of the trade unions." And it is true that bus drivers—in Birmingham, for instance—struck several times before accepting

West Indians as fellow employees; in other towns, transport workers have successfully insisted on a quota of colored workers. I have noted several cases in which a union has a closed- or union-shop agreement and by refusing to admit a West Indian to membership has denied him employment in the trade.

What explains this difference between principle and practice? Ask any individual worker this question and he will deny any prejudice. "It's not me," he will say, "it's the other blokes." I think there are three reasons for hesitation in accepting West Indians:

(1) There is the craftsman's conviction that they are not properly trained or skilled, and that they will thereby reduce trade standards.

(2) West Indians find it easiest to find jobs in industries that are acutely short of labor, such as public transport. The union members argue that such trades are short of recruits because wages and working conditions are not attractive enough. By admitting West Indians, therefore, they feel that they are weakening their bargaining power—and they suspect (wrongly) that West Indians are not very union conscious and cannot be relied on to strike.

(3) There is sexual jealousy and suspicion. Socially—as the futile effort to introduce Italians and refugee Poles into the coal mines has shown—this may be the most important though least articulate of the workers' objections.

Yet, despite these objections, West Indians are finding work, and they are now working their way up to more skilled jobs as they gain experience and so are proving that the suspicions are ill founded.

A Home of Their Own

Housing comes next to work as a problem for the West Indian immigrant. As new arrivals, very few of them can even get on the waiting lists for municipal houses or flats; they must go into lodgings—often owned by colored landlords—which are found most easily in the dingy and decaying streets that more prosperous workers are leaving. Colored workers, of course, do not "bring a district down" by moving into it; they can move into it just because it is already "coming down." That is what has happened in such London areas as Brixton, Paddington, and Camden Town. These "little Harlems" were near slums before the West Indians began to establish themselves, street by street.

Yet the familiar story repeats itself. Three years ago, in Baynes Street, Camden Town, there was a small race riot. And it took place just at the fringe of West Indian settlement. More and more colored immigrants are buying property, often on short leases or in poor condition, because this is easier than finding rented rooms in a white district. Recent surveys have shown that more than two thirds of sample groups of landladies refused to take colored people, and even some of those who were willing drew the line at "very dark men." And Dr. Senior quotes an analysis of the Kensington *Post* for August 22, 1955. From 260 advertisements offering accommodation, 46 discriminated against colored applicants. As he pointed out, a great many of the other vacancies would have been "full" if a colored man had turned up to seek the room. Yet he also quotes examples from five cities where West Indians have been employed on the bus system: in each case there was initial resistance, but the men were so polite and pleasant to passengers that it soon became easy to find accommodation for them.

There is, clearly, discrimination in housing, and the more immigrants who come, the more chance there is that housing—with social and recreational contact a close second—will prove to be the main point of friction.

The press can do much to increase or reduce friction of this kind. . . . In some cities, interracial committees have been set up to smooth the path of adjustment. There is a remarkably success-ful one in Leeds, where there are about fifteen hundred West Indians, which is called the Aggrey Society. It takes its name, and its motto from an African educationalist who said: "You can play a tune of sorts on the White keys and you can play a tune of sorts on the Black keys, but for harmony you must use both the Black and the White."

This society tries to meet colored people arriving in Leeds for the first time, providing them with temporary accommodation and helping them to find more permanent homes and jobs. There are similar groups and individuals in other towns, and the British Council of Churches last year sent out a memorandum to all clergymen advising them how best to help colored immigrants and to take the lead in minimizing racial problems. . . .

Dr. Senior suggested that a West Indian Welfare Office be set up in London, with sufficient staff to operate it effectively. Despite some timid objections to the effect that such an office might "scare" people in Britain and lead to hostile reaction, on June 1, 1956, a British Caribbean Welfare Service was opened in London, exactly along the lines of the Senior proposal.

Though none of the West Indian governments wishes to promote the migration of their skilled and semiskilled workers, they realize that the migration will go on while the disparity in conditions between the West Indies and Britain remains, and while no barriers are placed in the way of free movement. If, therefore, West Indians are going to migrate, everything possible should be done to prepare them for what lies ahead. They should be given precise information about the conditions that they will face in Britain—climate, wages, prices, job prospects, housing, social customs, and welfare legislation. In this way the migrant will at least know what to expect, and not be dependent upon the glowing advertisements of travel agencies, or upon the letters of relatives anxious to persuade the folks back home that they have made good across the Atlantic.

Proper liaison, moreover, will ensure that London has precise information about future arrivals and that steps are taken to look after them. In the past, even the welfare officers at the Colonial Office sometimes knew no more than a cable from the British consul in Marseilles or Genoa which ran something like this:

"Four hundred West Indians arrive Calais special train Wednesday morning."

Britain's color problem, then, has two parts. The first is how to meet the challenge of a substantial colored migration, how to reconcile the theory of equality that is accepted in principle and in law with the first practical test. Americans who have listened to British liberals laying down the law on their Negro problems may well watch with interest how the British react now that this is no longer a distant or abstract question.

The second part of the problem is what is to be done in the West Indies—a challenge that Britain has to face jointly with the local governments that want more independence and more economic help at the same time. Until there is some degree of population control in the West Indies, there is no long-term solution to this difficulty. There are only palliatives, and large-scale migration is one of them. It is not merely migration to Britain that is necessary: some must go to British Honduras and British Guiana, both potentially rich and largely unsettled territories. Some may even get to Brazil.

If West Indian migration to Britain has done nothing else, it has at least faced the British squarely with the plight of the Caribbean. The West Indian islands are now on the agenda of British politics. In the depression years before the war, the Welsh miners sang in the streets of London, and the shipyard workers of Jarrow hunger-marched on the capital. They made the more comfortable and prosperous counties of the South realize that something must be done to give work and hope to the depressed areas. Today, the West Indian migrant is playing a similar role. He is showing the British that the West Indies are the depressed area of contemporary Britain.

THE IRRESPONSIBLE SOCIETY [11]

I propose to discuss what I call the "irresponsible society," two aspects of it in particular. One relates to the problem of arbitrary economic power. Who behind the "decorous drapery of political democracy" (in Professor Tawney's phrase) has power, who really governs, who is and will be making the critical decisions that will influence the design and texture of social and economic life in the 1960's? My other theme concerns the

[11] From British Broadcasting Company talk by Richard M. Titmuss, professor of social administration, London School of Economics, and author of several influential books on social and economic policies. *Listener.* 114:207-9. Ag. 11, '60. Reprinted by permission.

position of the powerless groups in society: the dependent poor, the sick and disabled, the mentally afflicted, the feckless and the obscure. Both themes raise questions that cannot be asked—at least in public—in the Soviet Union. Boris Pasternak attempted to do so in *Doctor Zhivago* and was forced, poor man, to join the obscure.

If Western democracy means anything at all it must surely mean that we should be continually asking such questions and continually seeking the answers to them. And by answers I do not want to imply that we should stop short at passing legislation to limit, for example, the exercise of arbitrary power or to change the rules about national assistance. The framing of new laws in the field of social policy does not, as the British like to believe, necessarily solve the social problem. We have, in addition, therefore, to do a great many things to see that legislation is effective in increasingly bringing the forces of arbitrary economic power under public scrutiny and supervision. Similarly, we have to do a great many things over a long period of time if we wish to raise, more than proportionately, the quality of life of the under-privileged minorities. Well-intentioned welfare legislation does not, by itself, suffice. Nor is it enough, in an increasingly prosperous society, to claim, for instance, the the poorest fifth of the nation are sharing in this increased wealth. To take up such a position, to set this as our objective, can imply that in absolute terms we shall be accepting a society of more inequality; relatively more social injustice. We can too easily forget that in any society there are substantial sections of the population who have for many reasons an immunity to the processes of economic growth.

Moreover, in the scale of values that distinguishes the liberal democracies from the authoritarian states, to claim that we are richer than they are should not be, I submit, the fundamental test of the effectiveness and morality of different economic and social systems. What is fundamental is how we use and distribute our increasing affluence; the extent to which we collectively decide to deny ourselves to benefit others; and the degree to which we bring under public control the exercise of arbitrary economic power.

In the past half-century two of the great forces that have helped to sustain the debate about power and poverty in Britain have been war and mass unemployment. They have had more to do with the growth of the Labour party than the dogma of Victorian Marxism. They have tamed for long periods the appetites of Conservatives for inequality and élitism. If we assume, as we must in all faith assume for the purposes of social policy, that these forces have been banished, where do we look in future for the men, the movements, and the values that will continuously nourish the social conscience?

In America a number of thoughtful observers are now asking questions about the affluent society and the future of democracy. They have discovered that in a period of unprecedented economic growth the proportion of old people with low income—more than 50 per cent—was virtually the same in 1957 as in 1947. "We are breeding," it is said, "a new type of human being—a guy with a full belly, an empty mind, and a hollow heart." It is "the age of the shrug," dripping with fat, professional and trade-union selfishness, and social unconcern. It is made explicit in such books as *The Waist-High Culture* [by Thomas Griffith, an editor of *Time*].

During the past ten years the record in Britain of social inquiry and protest about power and poverty suggests that growing affluence may be having similar effects. Little has been done to redefine and restate in modern terms the inherent illogicalities and contradictions in the managerial capitalist system as it is developing within a changing social structure. We have signally failed to identify and study the new concentrations of economic and financial power which may threaten the rights and liberties of the subject to choose the values and decide the social priorities that will shape his society. While the large tax-free fortunes of the 1950's were being accumulated we made little effort to discover the real incidence of poverty and the standards of living among the old and other dependent groups. This, to me, is one of the more striking signs of the irresponsibility of the 1950's. In so far as a society fails to identify, by fact and not by inference, its contemporary and changing social problems it must expect its social conscience and its democratic values to languish. . . .

Who Uses the National Health Service?

There is little here to suggest that much progress has been made during the last ten years to concentrate help through the public services on those whose need is greatest. For all we know this conclusion may hold for other branches of the social services: medical care, education, housing and other welfare provisions. In terms of the quality and effectiveness of medical care (for the physically and mentally ill), who are the major beneficiaries of the National Health Service? We do not know: no official attempt has been made to find out who utilizes the Service, how often, in what sectors of cost and quality, and with what results. In the matter of housing, social workers could, ten years ago, quite hopefully put their more serious cases of hardship on council waiting lists. Now it is hopeless in many urban areas; waiting lists have either been abolished or remain as a polite administrative fiction. And many people believe that, without a revolution in local government and its financial resources, the new mental health provisions for community care will remain virtually a dead letter.

These illustrations of the retreat from government in the field of the traditional social services are indicative of what we may expect in the 1960's. Secretiveness in administration, an appalling lack of facts, the decline in quality of royal commissions and committees of inquiry have all combined to maintain much of the mythology of "the welfare state." Many of us must also now admit that we put too much faith in the 1940's in the concept of universality as applied to social security. Mistakenly, it was linked with economic egalitarianism. Those who have benefited most are those who have needed it least. We are only just beginning to see that the problems of raising the level of living, the quality of education, housing, and medical care of the poorest third of the nation calls for an immense amount of social inventiveness; for new institutional devices, new forms of cooperation, social control, ownership, and administration, and new ways of relating the citizen and consumer to services that intimately concern him. Social ideas may well be as important in Britain in the next half-century as technological innovation. . . .

Fringe Welfare

The annual value of fringe welfare today, including cheap stock options, may well exceed, if spread over working life, the salaries paid to the managerial, executive, and other classes. Their standard of living is doubled—or more than doubled. But it is mostly contingent welfare; the undivided loyalty tranquilizer of the corporation; the basis of a new monolithic society which, as Mr. Theodore Levitt has said of the American corporation, is on the way to becoming "a twentieth-century equivalent of the medieval church."

This leads me to my other theme and to consider recent trends in the concentration and combination of economic power. Simply for purposes of illustration I take as an example the power of the private insurance corporation. Here five big mergers took place . . . [in 1959] to reduce still further what little competition remains between these large-scale bureaucracies. The last decade has witnessed something of an explosion in the accumulation of immense funds in the hands of these insurance companies and pension trusts. The rate of growth in this control over the "economic surplus" may be even more dramatic in the next ten years. Though there are many causes, it is the relatively sudden impact and union of two major forces in Western society that has led to this explosion: demographic change and economic growth. No one who attempts to foresee the future of the public social services (to say nothing of economic freedom) in Britain, the U.S.A., and other countries can now ignore this development.

Although only meager information has been published it would seem, if we compare New York and London Stock Exchange lists, that the percentage holding of equities by British insurance companies and pension funds was in 1957 already more than double the percentage holding of common stock by their opposite numbers in the U.S.A. In other words, these institutions are twice as powerful in Britain as in America in terms of the ownership of industrial assets. More significant still is the rate of growth of these funds as a source of new capital. According to the Radcliffe Report [produced by a committee set up to study the working of the British monetary system] the insurance companies and pension funds "constitute by far the largest single source of new capital, the net rate of accumulation of the funds of the two groups of institutions being some £600 million per year." As investors, they now dominate the City.

We know virtually nothing about how this responsibility is exercised. The insurance companies even refused to disclose to the Radcliffe Committee the market value of their assets. Their freedom from public supervision and control was, according to one speaker at the 1957 Actuarial Congress in New York, "the envy of insurers in the stronghold of private enterprise."

Power Concentrated in Few Hands

This is one example of the growth of arbitrary power, a potential power, which can affect many important aspects of our economic life and our social values in the 1960's. It is power concentrated in relatively few hands, working at the apex of a handful of giant bureaucracies, technically supported by a group of professional experts, and accountable, in practice, to virtually no one. From other points of view it is a force making for greater centralization of decision-making power, reminding us again, as the Conservative party has recently done, of Disraeli's warning: "Centralization is the death blow of public freedom."

We do not know how this power is being used in terms of social welfare priorities or how far these massive investment funds are being or will be used to restore the outworn, mid-Victorian social capital of Britain. What we can only call "social policy decisions" are, however, continually being made, without any proper awareness or public discussion of what is involved in terms of the common good, and what consequences may flow from the choices made. It all goes on in what [Max] Weber [the German sociologist] described as "the secret sessions" of private bureaucratic power. "The 'secret,'" he added, "as a means of power, is, after all, more safely hidden in the books of an enterpriser than it is in the files of public authorities."

Underlying the notions of continued economic growth is the assumption of a dwindling role for government. One consequence is the muffling of social protest and the spread of conformity. Another is the growth of arbitrary financial and economic power. The public services are thus increasingly seen, as Professor John Kenneth Galbraith says, as an incubus; an unnecessary, doctrinaire burden on private enterprise. The act of affirmation, the positive political decision about equality and its correlate freedom, becomes harder to make as the majority of voters (and not just the top 10 per cent) grow richer. Negatively, they assume—in so far as they are helped to think about these matters at all—that the unseen mechanisms of a more prosperous market will automatically solve the problems of the poverty of dependency, the slums of obsolescence, the growth of irresponsible power, and all the contradictions that flow from undirected or misdirected social policies.

III. BRITAIN, EUROPE, AND THE COMMONWEALTH

EDITOR'S INTRODUCTION

At the end of the Second World War, Britain had the effective leadership of Western Europe. She was the only major European country which had emerged undefeated from the war and her prestige was extremely high. As a result, Europe looked to Britain for ideas throughout the latter part of the 1940's and the beginning of the 1950's. But Britain remained aloof, and a movement toward European unity began without her, a movement that culminated in the split of Europe into two rival trade blocs. These blocs, described in Don Cook's article, consist of the Six in the European Common Market, established in 1957 by the treaty of Rome—Belgium, France, Germany, Italy, Luxembourg, and the Netherlands; and the Seven in the European Free Trade Association, established in 1958 by the treaty of Stockholm —Austria, Britain, Denmark, Norway, Portugal, Sweden, and Switzerland. The policy of both the EFTA and the Common Market is to establish free trade among members; the Common Market, however, wishes to go further than the EFTA by having a common tariff against nonmembers and moving toward political confederation. Selwyn Lloyd's speech, the second article in this section, outlines the issues which caused the split between the Six and the Seven. Britain's stand could result in her comparative isolation. Recently, however, there have been some major concessions by Britain to meet the expressed views of the Six. .

Part of the hesitation in joining with Europe has resulted from Britain's traditional ties with what used to be called the Empire and is now called the Commonwealth. "The Structure and Meaning of the Commonwealth" explains her relationship to these countries. Britain has given freedom to a large part of her overseas possessions in the years since the war, and an impressively large number have chosen to remain associated with the Commonwealth. Nevertheless, not all observers believe that the Commonwealth is a really meaningful entity today; this view is reflected in the article "Will the British Commonwealth Hold Together?"

The next selection is taken from Prime Minister Harold Macmillan's speech to the Houses of Parliament in South Africa, a member of the Commonwealth until March 1961. In it he affirms Britain's devotion to the cause of freedom for the African territories and to racial equality—a position radically opposed to South African *apartheid* or strict separation of the races.

The decision of South Africa to leave the Commonwealth, following pressure by other members of the association to change her racial policies, represents a new departure. As the articles in this section make clear, the Commonwealth has previously been based on noninterference in the internal affairs of other members. It remains to be seen whether this departure from principle could be the first step toward the dissolution of the union.

The crux of the problem—whether Britain is to maintain herself as a leading world power, with an independent system of defense and with primary ties to the Commonwealth; or whether she is to join with others for military, economic, and political purposes—is defined in "Britain Faces a Major Shift." This last selection examines the choices Britain faces in policy and leads on to a consideration of the East-West conflict.

BRITAIN AND EUROPE AT SIXES AND SEVENS [1]

For a good many decades now, an attitude of detachment and faint distaste has been served up by successive British Foreign Secretaries, from Castlereagh to Eden, as the basis for Britain's "European policy."

From one generation to the next, it has been argued with logic, candor, and clarity that the correct and indeed the only possible role for Britain in Europe was to reject any kind of

[1] From article by Don Cook, chief correspondent for the European area, and former chief of the London bureau, New York *Herald Tribune. Reporter.* 21: 13-16. Jl. 9, '59. Reprinted by permission.

entangling partnership and instead—in the words of one famous Foreign Office memorandum by Sir Eyre Crowe in 1907— "throw her weight now in this scale and now in that, but ever on the side opposed to political dictatorship of the strongest single state or group at a given time."

To a remarkable degree it worked—so well, in fact, that it confronts the formulators of British foreign policy today with the fact that any other kind of "European policy" for Britain has become almost impossible politically. The story of British relations with Europe at the decisive moments of the last decade has, therefore, been a frustrating and unhappy record of rejected opportunities, lost opportunities, or opportunities which were finally acknowledged with too little enthusiasm, too late.

The plain fact is that British policy toward Europe, at this difficult moment for the West, has reached a dead end. Europe is split, with not even any distant signs of how the breach is to be repaired. Britain is in a position of isolation from its continental neighbors—economically, politically, and even in defense matters—and it is an isolation with nothing splendid about it. . . .

Change Versus Tradition

At the root of the problem of Britain and Europe lies the fact that while Europe has undergone a fundamental change in its internal relations in the last decade, Britain has clung to a traditional pattern of action that no longer successfully applies in the politics or economics of the postwar world.

To perceive how Britain stands vis-à-vis Europe today, contrast the situation when the war ended. All the elements of a dominant role in Western Europe were in Britain's hands. There was no Germany; France was distraught and chaotic. Britain stood supreme in military power and political prestige. Moreover, under Labour Foreign Secretary Ernest Bevin the British in fact got off to a glowing start in a new era of leadership in Europe. Bevin may not have conceived it that way, but he did seize the Marshall Plan offer "with both hands," as he put it later, and he did take the initiative that resulted in the creation of the Organization for European Economic Co-operation. And it was Bevin, too, who devised and pushed forward the Western European Union treaty that was the germ of the NATO alliance.

Though these were acts of a limited character in keeping with past British policy toward continental entanglements, they could have marked the beginnings of a growing and expanding British partnership with Europe. But as European recovery improved and political self-confidence came back, Europe began to forge ahead from these limited cooperative arrangements.

Europeans like Robert Schuman, Jean Monnet, Paul-Henri Spaak, Alcide de Gasperi, and Konrad Adenauer saw a new road opening before them—a casting off of old patterns of European nationalism, a gradual surrender of sovereignty, a growing merger of economic policies, in the end a politically united Europe. One by one, challenges presented themselves to Britain. And at each step of the way, no matter what the particular issues of politics or economics or military matters might have been, the challenge resolved to a simple question. It was: Europe is uniting—will you join?

The first big challenge came in 1951 with the Schuman Plan to pool Europe's coal and steel industries. Ernest Bevin was still Foreign Secretary, but he was a British Socialist before he was a European. To the Labour Government of that time, deeply engaged in its program of nationalizing the British economy, the Schuman Plan seemed to pose this question: Are we to surrender direction of our basic industry to a European High Authority, with powers to tell a British Socialist government how it is to plan a vital segment of the British economy? The Labour Government did not even think twice.

In 1953 and 1954, the same essential challenge of joining Europe again confronted Britain in the form of the European Defense Community treaty. But who would have expected the British General Staff—with its memories of the catastrophic days of May and June of 1940, when the French were pleading and demanding that the few remaining Royal Air Force squadrons be dispatched to the Continent—to merge the British forces, or even part of them, with a European Army?

In June 1955, Europe challenged again with the convening of the Messina Conference in Italy to begin work on a treaty for a European common market. Britain again was invited to join. Sir Anthony Eden, flushed with his May election victory, replied that there was no minister available but he could send a senior official. The European Six sent word back that it was a ministerial meeting, and if Britain couldn't find a minister to spare it could stay out.

From the small but deeply significant points of departure, the split between Britain and Europe on the economic front widened steadily, until it culminated in the acrimonious demise of the British Free Trade Area plan in Paris . . . [in December 1958].

The Free Trade Area plan represented a major effort by the British government to break the old pattern of policy and go well beyond anything previously attempted in "joining Europe." A Cabinet minister—Paymaster-General Reginald Maulding—was appointed to direct policy and conduct negotiations. With considerable energy he kept things moving. But it was a new experience for the British to realize that they needed Europe more than Europe needed Britain.

Although it was evident early in the game that the free trade plan involved a head-on clash of policy with the French, Britain continued to hope right down to the last months of 1958 that pressures from France's partners would produce a compromise between the Common Market and free trade. But in the end, the continental partners stuck together with France, and the Six refused to go further. Their contention was that the Free Trade Area plan was simply a device to get the economic advantages of the Common Market without a sacrifice of sovereignty.

The wrangle left a bitter aftertaste. After the rebuff, the British quietly patched up a temporary tariff and quota deal with France, but the Macmillan Cabinet came to the conclusion that it had gone as far as it could in the direction of Europe and that it was time to let the dust settle.

Logical and admirable as the Free Trade Area plan was, and laudable as it could have been as a means of preventing the division of non-Communist Europe into rival economic blocs, it had two fatal flaws. First, it was too much a reflection of British self-interest rather than a whole-hearted act of European partnership. Second, it again dodged that simple central issue of a symbolic surrender of sovereignty.

It was, in fact, almost as if someone in the Foreign Office, searching for an idea or a policy with which to meet the challenge of the European Common Market, had looked up that 1907 memorandum of Sir Eyre Crowe's—in which he also wrote:

Second only to the idea of independence, nations have always cherished the right of free intercourse and trade in the world's markets. In proportion as England champions the principle of the largest measure of general freedom of commerce, she undoubtedly strengthens her hold on the interested friendships of other nations—at least to the extent of making them feel less apprehensive of naval supremacy in the hands of a free-trade England than they would in the face of a predominant protectionist power. This is an aspect of the free trade question which is apt to be overlooked.

If it was good enough for Sir Eyre Crowe in 1907, it was certainly good enough for the Conservative Government in 1958. But it was not good enough for Europe.

This is the diplomatic road that has led to Stockholm [where the decision to set up the Free Trade Area was taken]. At every step of the way, the British position has been historically consistent and logical, and politically explainable. It has certainly been predictable. It may even have been "inevitable." But the fact remains that Europe has been in movement during this decade, and the British have failed to keep up with it. To be outdistanced in a race is to lose—and it is no good when the race is over saying that it was all the fault of the other fellow for running too fast.

Britain thus seems doomed by its decisions of the past ten years to spend a long period on the edge of Europe searching for opportunities and a policy. Unfortunately, Britain is more inclined to rationalize the position than face the import of the challenge.

Britain does not cease to be vulnerable to changes in Europe —up or down—simply by staying out. Moreover, the whole economic character of the Commonwealth has altered since the Ottawa preferential tariff agreements of 1933, and before another decade is out these agreements will be all but meaningless economically. [These agreements made trade between members of the Commonwealth attractive. Their favorable effect has been diminished by inflation.—Ed.]. . . [If] a slow decline to a "Little England" status is to be avoided, the British must be part of some wider and more expanding economic arrangement than they will ever achieve by clinging to the Commonwealth or relying on the Stockholm plans to do the job.

Britain's position as a world power is not based on sheer military strength, but rather on its capacity to lead and influence and direct. In the Bevin days of the Marshall Plan and the formation of the OEEC [Organization for European Economic Cooperation], Britain spoke for Europe and played the key role as a guiding force in European economic and political affairs. But in the circumstances its policy has helped bring about, Britain cannot aspire to regain its position of ten or twelve years ago in Europe. . . .

From the outside, there seems to be one simple answer to all this. Barbara Ward, former assistant editor of the *Economist,* is one of those who have proposed it:

The positive solution is to take the political and economic steps which enable Britain to influence European policies, and these, clearly, are now inconceivable outside the Common Market. By joining, the British restore themselves to the core of the great economic debate of our time. Britain cannot evade the issue by retiring from the arena in which it will be chiefly decided.

THE BRITISH POSITION [2]

That this House recognizes the need for political and economic unity in Europe, and would welcome the conclusion of suitable arrangements to that end, satisfactory to all the governments concerned. [Motion presented to the House of Commons.]

The motion seems to be simple and clear, but I could wish that it were as easy to make a simple and clear speech about it. The issues are complicated and public discussion of them has suffered from oversimplification. I will try to avoid that and also to avoid being overcomplicated.

The first matter mentioned in the motion is that of European unity, the need for political and economic unity in Europe. I want to make certain points absolutely clear. We in Britain regard ourselves as part of Europe. By history, by tradition, by civilization, by sentiment, by geography, we are part of Europe. At the Council of Europe, in Strasbourg, in January, I said that the fact that the English Channel had not been crossed successfully in war as often as had some other physical barriers in Europe did not disqualify us from European status. The fact that our Queen is head of the Commonwealth and that we are a member of that association does not disqualify us from European status. . . .

My first point is that if Britain were to be regarded as outside Europe we could not fulfill our complete role in the world. Nor do I believe that Europe would be complete without us.

My second point is with regard to the European Economic Community, the Six. We have, from the beginning, welcomed the formation of the Community of the Six as a step towards European unity. We welcome the economic strength and the political cohesion that the Community of the Six is bringing about. In particular, we welcome the new relationship which it embodies between France and Germany. But although we have welcomed the Six from the beginning, we have always

[2] From "Britain and Europe," speech by the Right Hon. Selwyn Lloyd, British Secretary of State for Foreign Affairs, before the House of Commons, July 25, 1960. British Information Services. 45 Rockefeller Plaza. New York 20. '60. Reprinted by permission.

been conscious of the danger that it might lead to a political division between us.

That point has repeatedly been made, and I will not elaborate it today except to say that in the present international situation everyone must be increasingly aware of the pressing need for unity in Western Europe. In seeking to avert this division we do not wish to affect the cohesion of the Six as an independent entity, or to prejudice the achievement by the Six of their political goal.

Faced with this problem of the possible division between the Six and the rest of Europe, we tried to solve the problem by putting forward in 1957, proposals for a European Free Trade Area. . . .

Because of the failure of those negotiations, it was natural that some countries outside the Six, who, during the negotiations, had shown that they were able and willing to adopt free trade arrangements, should act together, and this led to the formation of the European Free Trade Association—EFTA—by the Stockholm treaty.

We see three advantages in EFTA. First, it is an association of countries with populations of over ninety million, with high living standards, with highly developed industrial and agricultural skills, and it is in itself a powerful economic unit with great opportunities for expanding trade. Secondly, the formation into a group of these seven European countries has helped to preserve cohesion in the European economic system. I am sure that that will be proved to be so in any forthcoming negotiations. Thirdly, the successful negotiation of the treaty of Stockholm shows that it is possible for us to belong to a purely economic European association consistent with our Commonwealth membership.

Therefore, on this first matter, which is really the first part of the motion, I state categorically our wish for a united Europe, politically, economically and commercially. But there are different ways of attaining this. Some people talk of integration, others of federation, others of confederation, and others, again, of association. One is not any the less a good European because one prefers one method rather than another. Our purpose is a united Europe, and we accept the need for some political organization as an element in this unity. That being our objective, what are the problems and how should we seek to proceed?

First, the Commonwealth. I do not think that I need develop in this House the virtues and values of the Commonwealth relationship, the friendship and constant intimate exchange of views between peoples of many different races, amounting to a quarter of the population of the world. I believe that this relationship in the Commonwealth and this successful development of a multiracial association, is of great advantage not only to us but, also, to all our friends in Europe. The strength and cohesion of the Commonwealth is in part buttressed by its economic pattern, and we have a duty to see that no action of ours in the economic field endangers the immense political potential of this association.

That is where the first problem arises, because acceptance of a common tariff of the Six, as laid down in the treaty of Rome, would be the end of the principle of Commonwealth duty-free entry of goods and commodities. It would mean not only putting a tariff on the Commonwealth, but giving free entry to European producers and so a preference to them over the Commonwealth producers except for items on which the common tariff is nil. This would affect a large part of the Commonwealth sales in this country.

If, in addition, we adopted the common agricultural policy of the Six, embodying protection not only by tariffs but by various other means, this would be a further blow to one of the most important parts of Commonwealth trade. That is the first problem that we have to face. I do not for a moment say that it is insoluble, but it is a formidable problem.

The second problem is agriculture. The nature of the common agricultural policy which the Six propose, just as the kind of agricultural policies currently in operation in the individual countries of the Six, is basically different from our agricultural policy in the United Kingdom. Broadly speaking, theirs is a system under which the consumer pays the cost of farm support directly through the price of food in the shop. Ours is a system under which the cost of farm support is met directly by the Exchequer, and, therefore, by the taxpayer. As a result, we have much lower consumer prices in general than the Six. Indeed we have cheaper food than most countries in the world.

A switch to the system proposed by the European commission could have a severe impact on both the consumer and the producer in this country, and the extent of that impact could be uneven for different farm products, and its effects unpredictable. I think that a switch would involve for us fundamental readjustments in the farm support system, which, I think, has been recognized in this country as being best suited to our particular conditions. This is a problem which we shall have to consider very carefully before we make changes.

The third matter is our commercial relations with third countries. Under the treaty of Rome, apart from the question of the coordination of common policies within the Community, by 1970 members would have to abandon their direct commercial relations with third countries. In our case that would mean, amongst others, the countries of the Commonwealth, and the political consequences of such a development would be far-reaching. We have to remember that we do 84 per cent, I think it is, of our trade with countries outside the European Community, but, by their rules, by 1970 we would have to abandon our direct commercial relations with third countries.

There is also the question of the position of EFTA. We attach great importance to our membership of that association and we shall always act in the closest consultation with our EFTA partners. In loyalty to them we must ensure that any plan to secure political and economic unity in Europe takes care of their interests and their preoccupations and is formulated after full discussion with them.

The last problem I wish to raise is that of institutions. It is no use trying to burke this issue and to say that there is not a problem, because there is. What is not yet clear is how the institutions of the Six are to work out. For us, with our traditions in this Parliament, with the contribution it has made to parliamentary democracy, if the plan is to make this Parliament subordinate to some higher parliament, it is no light matter.

The relationship of Parliament to other international institutions requires very careful consideration. It is difficult to be more specific in the absence of knowledge as to the precise powers of such a higher parliament, or assembly. I can say only this: if the higher parliament were to control the whole social and economic life of the people, the fiscal policies, the financial systems, the commercial policies, I think that we, as parliamentarians, would have to think very carefully about what our position would be. The abdication of our powers on these issues is not a matter lightly to be brushed aside. . . .

That being our view, what do we do in the immediate future? I shall try to put before the House what I think is the course of action we should take. First, we have to develop in every way we can our trade and other relations with EFTA. As I have already said, there are many promising opportunities there. Secondly, there is no reason why EFTA trade with the Six should not expand, in view of the general prosperity in Europe. This will be our aim and I am not at all sure that there is not a little too much defeatism in some quarters about the future of our trade with the Six.

Next, it is in our interest from every point of view to try to reduce so far as possible the discrimination between the two groups and to play a full part in the GATT [General Agreement on Trade and Tariffs] conference this winter in order to bring about a useful reduction in the level of world tariffs. In addition, and perhaps the most important of all, we have to do all in our power to strengthen the political will in Western Europe directly towards achieving satisfactory and suitable arrangements. Without it, there will not be "suitable arrangements"—the words in the motion—but with that will sufficiently strong there are bound to be satisfactory arrangements.

A great deal is going on in this direction. There is a considerable movement of parliamentary opinion in Europe. All . . . members, on both sides of the House, who have been in touch with this European parliamentary opinion know that there is a developing pressure for agreement, a pressure which I whole-heartedly welcome. . . .

I fully agree that this involves a political relationship just as much as an economic relationship, but both those relationships must depend upon the kind of solutions which may be found possible to the problems and difficulties which I have outlined. When we talk of suitable arrangements, I certainly would not exclude participation in common institution. Therefore, in the absence of discussion of long-term problems with the Six, the courses which I have set out today are what it is best for us to do.

We recognize, however, that none of these courses is a full substitute for a thoroughgoing European solution. In the present state of the world—the current difficulties in East-West relations, the explosive happenings in Africa, the dangers elsewhere —it is obvious that Western Europe must come closer together. I therefore ask the House to state in the clearest possible terms that we recognize the need for political and economic unity in Europe and would welcome the conclusion of suitable arrangements to that end satisfactory to all the governments concerned. We, for our part, are prepared to work wholeheartedly for that conclusion.

THE STRUCTURE AND MEANING OF THE COMMONWEALTH [3]

The Commonwealth comprises not only the United Kingdom and the other independent member countries (previously known as Dominions), but a variety of territories at different stages of constitutional development which are partly or wholly dependent upon the United Kingdom and other of the member countries.

The first classic definition of the status of, and of the relationship between, the United Kingdom and the Dominions (as they were then known) was contained in the Balfour Declaration, which was drawn up subsequent to the imperial conference of 1926. This referred to the United Kingdom,

[3] From "The Commonwealth." *British Affairs*. 3:194-8. D. '59. Reprinted by permission.

Canada, Australia, New Zealand and South Africa (as well as the Irish Free State, which subsequently left the Commonwealth, and Newfoundland, which has now become a province of Canada) as "autonomous communities within the British Empire, equal in status, in no way subordinate one to another in any aspect of their domestic or external affairs, though united by a common allegiance to the Crown and freely associated as members of the British Commonwealth of Nations." It is important to remember that, although imperial conferences of this period were concerned to define an intra-Commonwealth relationship (which in practice already existed), no attempt was made then or at any subsequent time to lay down a constitution for the British Commonwealth.

Constitutional Links

The constitutional development of the dependencies of Commonwealth governments is a matter lying solely within the discretion of the member country concerned. For example, the question when Nigeria (or Samoa) should be granted independence is one for the United Kingdom (or New Zealand) alone to decide. But the further question whether Nigeria (or Samoa), once independent, should be accepted as a fellow member of the Commonwealth is one for decision by all the existing independent members of the Commonwealth.

The Commonwealth possesses no common structure. Its members are not all bound together by formal treaties, alliances or obligations. There is no central control of foreign or economic policy. It is what it describes itself as being—a free association of wholly independent and equal states. Nevertheless individual members of the Commonwealth have joined regional organizations such as NATO and SEATO and thus found themselves in alliance with other Commonwealth members. In addition on first attaining independence and being without adequate defense forces of their own some Commonwealth governments have signed defense agreements with Britain. Beyond this there is no common defense policy.

The Common Interest

The essence of the association, however, is to provide a means of discussing issues of common interest. It is an accepted convention of this association that no member should interfere in the internal affairs of another member, and that no member should discuss with another member the internal affairs and internal policies of a third member. Equally it is an accepted convention that, so far as is possible, no member shall embark upon a course of action known to affect the interests of another member without prior consultation—but members are entirely free to take their own decisions, and serious divergencies of opinion have on occasion arisen when members agreed to differ on certain issues.

With the exception of Canada, all members are members of the sterling area. (The sterling area also includes some other countries not within the Commonwealth.) There is thus a general interest in maintaining and strengthening sterling as an international currency, since the bulk of the international reserves of the rest of the sterling area are held in sterling. But all members of the sterling area have full control over their sterling holdings and are free to draw upon the gold and dollar reserves held centrally by Britain. Britain operates no exchange control over current or capital transactions by the rest of the sterling area with the outside world, though, in the overriding interests of maintaining the strength of the pound, the latter adopt exchange control policies similar to those of the United Kingdom. Thus the United Kingdom's consent was not required, nor was it sought when the Ghana government decided to make a credit of £10 million available to the government of Guinea.

Similarly each member of the Commonwealth is free to adopt its own policy in economic matters. Under the Commonwealth or imperial preference system, Commonwealth countries concede certain trade advantages to one another. Britain for example allows duty-free entry to most Commonwealth goods; some other Commonwealth countries grant certain margins of preference to goods manufactured in Britain and elsewhere in the Commonwealth. But there is no central agreement nor is there central direction: Commonwealth countries are autonomous in tariff matters. The essence of the system is reciprocity, and the system is based on a series of bilateral agreements between the countries concerned.

Consultation

The Commonwealth thus maintains a continuous exchange of views on issues affecting foreign and economic policy. At the day-to-day level, these exchanges are conducted through the Commonwealth Relations Service (see below). They are reinforced by a multiplicity of standing committees set up to deal with specialized topics. On occasion, special meetings of representatives of Commonwealth governments are called to consider urgent or important issues—e.g., periodic discussions of general objectives of economic policy—but agreements reached at these meetings are not mandatory on individual members. And at the highest level meetings of Commonwealth ministers are held to review and discuss major policy questions—finance ministers usually meet once a year, prime ministers at somewhat less frequent intervals. The basis of all such consultation and discussion is that of voluntary cooperation. Any attempt by any member to impose common policies on the other members would be fruitless and, if persistently attempted, would inevitably weaken what the president of India has described as "the silken bond around the Commonwealth."

The Commonwealth Relations Service is the agency by which the United Kingdom's part in the continuous process of consultation and cooperation is carried on, and by which Government business with other Commonwealth countries is mainly conducted. Its ministerial head is the Secretary of State for Commonwealth Relations. The Service consists of the Commonwealth Relations Office in London and of the United Kingdom High Commissioners' Offices in other countries of the Commonwealth. Its work is largely diplomatic in character and covers all aspects of United Kingdom policy, particularly in external affairs. In effect, and subject to the particularly close relations between the Commonwealth governments, the functions of the Commonwealth Relations Office are in general similar to those of the Foreign Office, with which the Commonwealth Relations Office works always in close association.

As regards relations with countries outside the Commonwealth, each member maintains its own diplomatic service, and most of them have their own ambassadors in various foreign countries. Where a member is not so represented, the United Kingdom ambassador in the foreign country concerned represents the interests of the Commonwealth country to the extent that the government of the latter country desires. It is, however, open to any such member of the Commonwealth to adopt other channels of communication if it thinks fit. In some instances this takes the form of communication between the High Commissioner for the Commonwealth country in London and the ambassador of the foreign country also in London.

The Queen's Representative

Since the Queen is normally resident in the United Kingdom, the majority of the constitutional functions which she performs in the United Kingdom, such as the appointment of Cabinet ministers, the summoning and dissolution of Parliament and the assent to legislation passed by the legislature, are performed in those countries of which Her Majesty is Queen by a governor-general on her behalf. In many instances he is a citizen of the country concerned but, even if he is a United Kingdom citizen, he is in no way a representative of the United Kingdom Government, but is solely Her Majesty's representative and in all public affairs he acts, as the Queen does in Britain, on the advice of his ministers. He is appointed on the advice of the government of the country concerned. Where any executive action is taken by the Queen herself either in Britain or on the occasion of a visit to another Commonwealth country, ministers of that country tender their advice direct to Her Majesty and *not* through United Kingdom ministers who are in no way concerned in such a matter. The representative of the United Kingdom Government in a member country of the Commonwealth is, as indicated above, a high commissioner whose functions are generally similar to those of an ambassador in a foreign country.

WILL THE BRITISH COMMONWEALTH HOLD TOGETHER? [4]

Great Britain is discovering that the Commonwealth of Nations which once represented the greatest power in the world really doesn't amount to very much any more.

This is the shock which most people in Britain just now are absorbing:

Britain can no longer dominate the Commonwealth, can no longer protect it, can no longer count on all of its members' standing by its side if Britain goes to war.

So loose are the bonds of the Commonwealth that there is not even any joint military command. Nor is there joint strategic planning.

Even the marketing agreements between Commonwealth countries are so strained, so shot through with exceptions and difficulties, that many Britons feel that they would fare better without them and are prepared to give up the whole preferential system.

The Commonwealth of peoples of all races, once ruled by whites, now is a much divided group of nations, ruled—in the majority—by nonwhites.

Even the British crown, once a unifying force, is losing some of its luster. Three of the ten Commonwealth nations no longer recognize the reigning British monarch as chief of their governments. Several other members are preparing to abandon this formality.

[4] From article in *U.S. News & World Report.* 48:80-1. My. 9, '60. Reprinted from *U.S. News & World Report*, an independent weekly news magazine published at Washington. Copyright 1960 United States News Publishing Corporation.

All of these changes are coming to the surface as Britain . . . seeks to avert a showdown that could tear apart the loosely joined federation.

The crisis now [May 1960] confronting the Commonwealth is highlighted by major racial troubles in one of the member nations—South Africa. [South Africa withdrew from the Commonwealth in March 1961.—Ed.] But there is more to the problem than that. . . .

What fifteen years ago was exclusively a white man's "club" has evolved into an association dominated by nonwhites—Asians and Africans. In other ways, too, this institution has undergone a transformation.

Before World War II, the Commonwealth was made up exclusively of "white" dominions—Canada, Australia, New Zealand and South Africa. These were governed, in the main, by people of British stock who retained their loyalty to the British monarchy. Many of them regarded Britain as their mother country.

The nations of the old Commonwealth looked to Britain for their defense. When Britain declared war on Germany in 1939, the Commonwealth followed almost automatically. Only South Africa hesitated—first debating and then defeating a proposal that it remain neutral.

The New Commonwealth

Take a look at the new Commonwealth as it has grown up since World War II. As the British colonial empire has shrunk, the Commonwealth has expanded. Every colony that gained independence, with the single exception of Burma, has chosen to throw in its lot with the Commonwealth.

There is no constitution for the Commonwealth and there are no membership rules. It is just assumed that any British colony will be accepted into the Commonwealth when it becomes free.

There are now as many nonwhite member nations as there are white members. When Nigeria joins the group in October

[1960] the nonwhites will have a majority. As more and more British colonies gain independence over the next few years, the nonwhite members will become steadily more predominant.

As for population, the whites are heavily outnumbered—fewer than 100 million whites against more than 500 million Asians and Africans.

Few of these nonwhite "citizens" of the Commonwealth pay allegiance to Britain's Queen Elizabeth. India and Pakistan have become republics. Ghana has voted to adopt a republican form of government, too. Ceylon is planning a similar move. Malaya has formed a monarchy of its own.

If Britain should go to war, it could not count on support from all its Commonwealth partners, as in the past. Britain lacks the power to guarantee the defenses of its fellow members. This country is heavily dependent on the United States for the defense of its home islands. So each of the Commonwealth countries—new and old—is making its own defense arrangements.

The United States, to some degree, is replacing Britain as military protector of the Commonwealth.

Australia and New Zealand have joined a defense pact with the United States—known as ANZUS—that does not include Britain. They have also joined another United States-sponsored alliance—the Southeast Asian Treaty Organization [SEATO]—aimed at curbing Chinese Communist aggression in Southeast Asia, backdoor to Australia and New Zealand. Britain also is a member of SEATO.

Canada collaborates closely with the United States on defense matters. There is a joint Canadian-American air defense arrangement, and defense planning in other areas is close.

Pakistan is the only nonwhite member of the Commonwealth that is collaborating with the United States on defense. America has been supplying that country with military equipment on a large scale. Pakistan also is a member of SEATO.

India, pursuing a policy of neutralism, has made it clear that it relies tacitly on the United States to give aid in any emergency. India is no longer willing to supply Britain with the masses of soldiers that helped this country hold the Empire together for so many decades.

All these far-reaching changes in the Commonwealth are causing people in Britain to ask such searching questions as these:

What really holds the Commonwealth together? Why do British colonies, as they become independent, find it worthwhile to stay in the Commonwealth? And what are the advantages for Britain?

It is the profit motive, more than anything else, that has drawn the countries together. Economic advantages are mutual to the former colonies and to Britain. Take trade, for example:

Combined, the Commonwealth countries form Britain's biggest market and her biggest source of imports. Altogether, they account for 45 per cent of this country's foreign trade.

It works the other way, too. Britain is the most important trading partner of all the Commonwealth nations except Canada, which has strong economic ties with the United States.

Also, there is important trade between other Commonwealth countries on their own. For example, 55 per cent of Australia's trade is with members of the Commonwealth family. The Commonwealth's tariff preference system expedites a massive exchange of goods.

For Britain and some other Commonwealth countries, however, this system of tariff preferences, while still valuable, is proving to be a wasting asset. A continuing inflation is absorbing the real benefits of tariff concessions.

Looking closely at this international alliance, you find that the Commonwealth countries still have some sentimental and economic ties with Britain. Yet, more and more its members look to the United States for defense, for credit and aid and for political leadership.

Is the Commonwealth then likely to disintegrate? Most experts . . . say not. On the contrary, they say, the Commonwealth almost certainly will pick up additional members in the years just ahead, as more British colonies become independent. But the days of the old white man's "club" definitely are history.

COMMONWEALTH INDEPENDENCE
AND INTERDEPENDENCE [5]

It is a great privilege to be invited to address the members of both Houses of Parliament in the Union of South Africa. It is a unique privilege to do so in 1960 just half a century after the Parliament of the Union came to birth. I am most grateful to you all for giving me this opportunity and I am especially grateful to your Prime Minister who invited me to visit this country and arranged for me to address you here today. My tour of Africa, parts of Africa, the first ever made by a British Prime Minister in office is now also nearing its end but it is fitting that it should culminate in the Union Parliament here in Cape Town, in this historic city so long Europe's gateway to the Indian Ocean. . . .

No one could fail to be impressed with the immense material progress which has been achieved. That all this has been accomplished in so short a time is a striking testimony to the skill, energy and initiative of your people. We in Britain are proud of the contribution we have made to this remarkable achievement. Much of it has been financed by British capital. According to the recent survey made by the Union government nearly two thirds of the oversea investment outstanding in the Union at the end of 1956 was British. That is after two staggering wars which have bled our economy white. . . .

As I have traveled round the Union I have found everywhere, as I expected, a deep preoccupation with what is happening in the rest of the African continent. I understand and sympathize with your interest in these events, and your anxiety about them. Ever since the breakup of the Roman Empire one of the constant facts of political life in Europe has been the emergence of independent nations. They have come into existence over the centuries in different forms, with different kinds of government, but all have been inspired by a deep, keen feeling of nationalism which has grown as the nations have grown.

[5] From address by the Right Hon. Harold Macmillan, Prime Minister, delivered before both Houses of Parliament of the Union of South Africa, Cape Town, February 3, 1960. Text from *Vital Speeches of the Day*. 26:290-4. Mr. 1, '60.

Wind of Change in Africa

In the twentieth century and especially since the end of the war the processes which gave birth to the nation-states of Europe have been repeated all over the world. We have seen the awakening of national consciousness in peoples who have for centuries lived in dependence upon some other power. Fifteen years ago this movement spread through Asia. Many countries there of different races and civilizations pressed their claim to an independent national life. Today the same thing is happening in Africa, and the most striking of all the impressions I have formed since I left London a month ago is of the strength of this African national consciousness. In different places it takes different forms, but it is happening everywhere. The wind of change is blowing through this continent, and whether we like it or not this growth of national consciousness is a political fact. We must all accept it as a fact, and our national policies must take account of it.

Of course you understand this better than anyone. You are sprung from Europe, the home of nationalism, and here in Africa you have yourselves created a new nation. Indeed in the history of our times yours will also be recorded as the first of the African nationalisms, and this tide of national consciousness which is now rising in Africa is a fact for which you and we and the other nations of the Western world are ultimately responsible. For its causes are to be found in the achievements of Western civilization, in the pushing forward of the frontiers of knowledge, in the applying of science, in the service of human needs, in the expanding of food production, in the speeding and multiplying of means of communication, and perhaps, above all more than anything else, the spread of education.

Significance of the Growth of National Consciousness

As I have said, the growth of national consciousness in Africa is a political fact and we must accept it as such. That means, I would judge, that we must come to terms with it. I sincerely believe that if we cannot do so we may imperil the precarious balance between the East and the West on which the peace of the world depends. The world today is divided into three main groups. First there are what we call the Western powers. You in South Africa and we in Britain belong to this group together with our friends and allies in other parts of the Commonwealth. In the United States of America and in Europe we call it the free world. Secondly there are the Communists, Russia and her satellites in Europe and China whose population will rise by the end of the next ten years to the staggering total of 800 million. Thirdly there are those parts of the world whose people are at present uncommitted either to Communism or to our Western ideas.

In this context we think first of Asia and of Africa. As I see it the great issue in this second half of the twentieth century is whether the uncommitted peoples of Asia and Africa will swing to the East or to the West. Will they be drawn into the Communist camp? Or will the great experiments in self-government that are now being made in Asia and Africa, especially within the Commonwealth, prove so successful and by their example so compelling, that the balance will come down in favor of freedom and order and justice?

Responsibility of Commonwealth Members for Own Policy

The struggle is joined and it is a struggle for the minds of men. What is now on trial is much more than our military strength or our diplomatic and administrative skill. It is our way of life. The uncommitted nations want to see before they choose. What can we show them to help them choose right? Each of the independent members of the Commonwealth must answer that question for itself. It is a basic principle of our modern Commonwealth that we respect each other's sovereignty in matters of internal policy. At the same time we must recognize that in this shrinking world in which we live today the internal policies of one nation may have effects outside it. We may sometimes be tempted to say to each other "Mind your own business," but in these days I would myself expand the old saying so that it runs "Mind your own business but mind how it affects my business, too."

British Policy

Let me be very frank with you, my friends. What governments and parliaments in the United Kingdom have done since the war in according independence to India, Pakistan, Ceylon, Malaya and Ghana and what they will do for Nigeria and other countries now nearing independence—all this, though we take full and sole responsibility for it, we do in the belief that it is the only way to establish the future of the Commonwealth and of the free world on sound foundations. All this of course is also of deep and close concern to you, for nothing we do in this small world can be done in a corner or remain hidden. What we do today in West, Central and East Africa becomes known tomorrow to everyone in the Union whatever his language, color or traditions. Let me assure you, in all friendliness, that we are well aware of this and that we have acted and will act with full knowledge of the responsibility we have to all our friends. Nevertheless I am sure you will agree that in our own areas of responsibility we must each do what we think right. What we think right derives from a long experience both of failure and success in the management of our own affairs.

We have tried to learn and apply the lessons of both our judgment of right and wrong and our justice is rooted in the same soil as yours—in Christianity and in the rule of law as the basis of a free society. This experience of our own explains why it has been our aim in the countries for which we have borne responsibility, not only to raise the material standards of living but to create a society which respects the rights of individuals, a society in which men are given the opportunity to grow to their full stature, and that must in our view include the opportunity to have an increasing share in political power and responsibility, a society in which individual merit and individual merit alone is the criterion for a man's advancement, whether political or economic.

Finally, in countries inhabited by several different races it has been our aim to find means by which the community can become more of a community, and fellowship can be fostered between its various parts. This problem is by no means confined to Africa nor is it always a problem of a European minority. In Malaya, for instance, though there are Indian and European minorities, Malays and Chinese make up the great bulk of the population, and the Chinese are not much fewer in numbers than the Malays. Yet these two people must learn to live together in harmony and unity and the strength of Malaya as a nation will depend on the different contributions which the two races can make.

The attitude of the United Kingdom towards this problem was clearly expressed by the Foreign Secretary, Mr. Selwyn Lloyd, speaking at the United Nations General Assembly on the 17th September 1959. These were his words:

> In those territories where different races or tribes live side by side the task is to ensure that all the people may enjoy security and freedom and the chance to contribute as individuals to the progress and well-being of these countries. We reject the idea of any inherent superiority of one race over another.

Our policy, therefore is nonracial. It offers a future in which Africans, Europeans, Asians, the peoples of the Pacific, and others with whom we are concerned will all play their full part as citizens in the countries where they live, and in which feelings of race will be submerged in loyalty to new nations.

Special Problems of South Africa

I have thought you would wish me to state plainly and with full candor the policy for which we in Britain stand. It may well be that in trying to do our duty as we see it we shall sometimes make difficulties for you. If this proves to be so we shall regret it. But I know that even so you would not ask us to flinch from doing our duty. You too will do your duty as you see it. I am well aware of the peculiar nature of the problems with which you are faced here in the Union of South Africa. I know the differences between your situation and that of most of the other states in Africa. You have here some three million people of European origin. This country is their home. It has been their home for many generations. They have no other.

The same is true of Europeans in Central and East Africa. In most other African states those who have come from Europe have come to work, to contribute their skills, perhaps to teach but not to make a home.

The problems to which you as members of the Union Parliament have to address yourselves are very different from those which face the parliaments of countries with homogeneous populations. There are complicated and baffling problems. It would be surprising if your interpretation of your duty did not sometimes produce very different results from ours in terms of government policies and actions.

As a fellow member of the Commonwealth it is our earnest desire to give South Africa our support and encouragement, but I hope you won't mind my saying frankly that there are some aspects of your policies which make it impossible for us to do this without being false to our own deep convictions about the political destinies of free men to which in our own territories we are trying to give effect. I think we ought as friends to face together, without seeking to apportion credit or blame, the fact that in the world of today this difference of outlook lies between us. . . .

Interdependence of Nations

The fact is that in this modern world no country, not even the greatest, can live for itself alone. Nearly two thousand years ago when the whole of the civilized world was comprised within the confines of the Roman Empire, St. Paul proclaimed one of the great truths of history—we are all members one of another. During this twentieth century that eternal truth has taken on a new and exciting significance. It has always been impossible for the individual man to live in isolation from his fellows, in the home, the tribe, the village, or the city; today it is impossible for nations to live in isolation from one another. What Dr. John Donne said of individual men three hundred years ago is true today of my country, your country and all the countries of the world. "Any man's death diminishes me because I am involved in mankind; and therefore never send to know for whom the bell tolls; it tolls for thee." All nations now are interdependent one upon another and this is generally realized throughout the Western world. I hope in due course the countries of communism will recognize it too. . . .

In conclusion may I say this. I have spoken frankly about the differences between our two countries in their approach to one of the great current problems with which each has to deal within its own sphere of responsibility. These differences are well known. They are matters of public knowledge, indeed of public controversy, and I should have been less than honest if by remaining silent on them I had seemed to imply that they did not exist. But differences on one subject, important though it is, need not and should not impair our capacity to cooperate with one another in furthering the many practical interests which we share in common.

The independent members of the Commonwealth do not always agree on every subject. It is not a condition of their association that they should do so. On the contrary the strength of our Commonwealth lies largely in the fact that it is a free association of independent sovereign states, each responsible for ordering its own affairs but cooperating in the pursuit of common aims and purposes in world affairs. Moreover these differences may be transitory. In time they may be resolved. Our duty is to see them in perspective against the background of our long association.

BRITAIN FACES A MAJOR SHIFT [6]

Britain right now is in the midst of making three momentous decisions that will determine the role that this country is to play in world affairs for the next fifty years.

[6] From "Looking for New Role in World—Britain Faces Major Shift." *U.S. News & World Report.* 48:52-3. F. 8, '60. Reprinted from *U.S. News & World Report,* an independent weekly news magazine published at Washington. Copyright 1960 United States News Publishing Corporation.

The decisions are these:

Decision No. 1—Defense. Should Britain try to maintain her own, independent nuclear strength at a back-breaking cost in order to retain recognition as a great military power? Or should she share her nuclear weapons with her European allies to create a "European nuclear deterrent"?

Decision No. 2—Europe. Should Britain remain aloof from the "new" Europe that is now taking shape around France and West Germany, thereby risking the loss of British markets and influence? Or should this country somehow join this new European power bloc, even if it means altering Britain's special ties with the United States and the British Commonwealth?

Decision No. 3—African Empire. Should the remnants of Britain's Empire in Africa be liquidated quickly by turning them over to native rule? Or should the privileged position of the white minorities in the African colonies be defended at the risk of a series of crises like the one the French now face in Algeria?

While these important decisions are taking shape, a casual American visitor in London would hardly notice that anything out of the ordinary is happening here. No one is talking about history-making issues coming to a head. Everything seems normal. That's the way things are handled here. On the surface, it looks like a typical case of British "muddling through.". . .

The change [in prospect] is from the position of a great world power, with a globe-girdling empire, to that of an island nation dependent almost entirely upon its own resources and ingenuity.

Britain's richest colonies are already gone. So, too, is her former military dominance. Now, for a small country, the cost of membership in the "great-power club" is becoming prohibitive. Therefore, British statesmen are being forced to chart a new course.

Right now, the African problem is the most immediate. A dangerous crossroads has been reached. Britain must choose between white supremacy or black rule in her remaining colonies.

Previously, in the step-by-step liquidation of Britain's African empire, this issue had not arisen because the white population was negligible or politically impotent in the colonies that were given or promised their independence.

But now comes Kenya. The white minority there numbers 65,000. Many of the whites have vast holdings of land. They are fighting bitterly to prevent any move by the British Government that would lead to black rule in Kenya.

Kenya's 6.5 million natives, however, are demanding self-rule this year, and their fiery young leader, Tom Mboya, is insisting that the government be elected on the principle of "one man, one vote." That would mean black rule.

The showdown on Kenya is at hand, in a conference between British and Kenya representatives that began [in January 1960] in London. . . . [The result was a compromise which really satisfied no one.—Ed.]

A similar crisis is to face British policy makers later this year when a conference is to be held in London to consider the future of the Central African Federation, made up of Southern Rhodesia, Northern Rhodesia and Nyasaland. More than 300,000 white settlers there pose a serious problem. [Once again, the resulting compromise satisfied none of the parties concerned.—Ed.]

In Europe, Britain has reached another turning point. In the past, Britain has remained aloof from the Continent, playing one power off against another. But the rise of Communist Russia has transformed the situation. A unified Western Europe is considered vital to British security today.

Yet, as Western Europe unites around the Common Market, Britain sees a danger of being shut out of Europe's great market place and—equally important—losing its influence in European politics. [See the first two articles in this section, above.—Ed.]

A new policy on Europe, therefore, is taking shape here in London.

Basically, Britain has decided to join the new Europe—but in collaboration with the United States. The question is how this can best be done.

What Britain is turning toward is a course of following the United States lead in creating a new economic organization for

Europe—one with full United States and Canadian participation. . . . [The Organization for European Economic Cooperation and Development, with the United States, Canada, and . . . eighteen European countries as members, has been brought into existence, subject to acceptance by national parliaments.—Ed.]

The strategy that appears to be emerging from the three great decisions that the British now face is this: Britain will speed the liquidation of her Empire and draw closer to Europe in a new kind of partnership which will include the United States.

IV. NUCLEAR POWER AND THE EAST-WEST CONFLICT

EDITOR'S INTRODUCTION

In the years since the end of the war, Britain has had to adjust to being in effect one of the second-ranking powers in the world. Although Britain emerged from the war as one of the Big Five, it rapidly became clear that in a world of rampant military technology only two nations, America and Russia, could command the resources to be major powers. Indeed, there are now commentators who suggest that even Russia and America no longer possess meaningful power, since they can use their power only at an unacceptable cost. In addition, whatever may be the views about the possibility of meaningful civil defense in a vast country like America or Russia, Britain must accept the fact that even a small number of thermonuclear weapons would be sufficient to blast her out of existence.

For this reason, there is a large, and probably growing, segment of British opinion which supports unilateral nuclear disarmament. The first three articles in this section discuss the meaning and direction of the movement toward this goal, examining the problem from three different viewpoints. In "British Still Hope for 1961 Summit" we see why the British Government, realizing the "impossibility" of war, favors negotiation to reduce tensions. The final selection, "Prospects of Mankind," is the report of a debate between several recognized leaders of world opinion; it draws together many of the threads of the discussion that is now going on throughout the world.

THE CAMPAIGN FOR NUCLEAR DISARMAMENT [1]

On Easter Mondays, Admiral Nelson usually looks down from his pillar onto a Trafalgar Square filled by tourists and

[1] From "British Opinion Marches," by Norman Birnbaum, an American sociologist teaching in England at the time this article was written, who participated in the march he describes. *Nation.* 188:337-9. Ap. 18, '59. Reprinted by permission.

pigeons. This year [1959], however, he saw 15,000 demonstrators march into the square to the applause of some 10,000 spectators. In the largest demonstration since the war (some say since the turn of the century), these thousands gave concrete expression to the protest of millions against their country's continuing preparation for participation in a nuclear conflict.

The march actually began on Good Friday, outside the gates of Britain's Los Alamos, the Atomic Weapons Research Establishment at Aldermaston in Berkshire, fifty-three miles from London. Its organizers, the Campaign for Nuclear Disarmament, . . . staged a march [in 1958] from London to Aldermaston; a hard core of 500 marchers, joined on the first and last days by some 3,500 others, had covered the distance—to derisive notices from the press and a public response either apathetic or hostile. This year, to the . . . surprise of the organizers, things were different: 5,000 began the march and the numbers at no time dipped below 3,000. On the last day, we set out from the western part of the city (on the road in from London Airport), 5,500 strong; this figure doubled by the lunch break in Hyde Park, and on the final leg through Whitehall to Trafalgar Square another 5,000 came off the sidewalks to join. [In 1960, 100,000 people met in Trafalgar Square under the same auspices.—Ed.] Nothing succeeds like success: the press changed its tone, and even . . . the BBC [British Broadcasting Corporation] paid us some attention.

The Campaign for Nuclear Disarmament is explicitly non-political. Its heads are Canon John Collins of St. Paul's Cathedral . . . ; Bertrand Russell; the historian A. J. P. Taylor; the novelist, J. B. Priestley; the Labour politician and journalist, Michael Foot. It has mobilized that most effective but most naked of all political weapons, the human conscience. Its organization and propaganda methods are amateurish, but this may be an advantage: it has capitalized on the widespread disgust many feel with the overorganized opportunism of both major parties. It has two arguments: (1) that nuclear war means the extirpation of life in these islands; (2) that nuclear weapons are profoundly immoral. It has but one concrete proposal:

unilateral British renunciation of nuclear weapons. These primitive political propositions have enabled the CND, if the evidence of the demonstration is to be believed, to strike deep roots in the populace. . . .

The failure of both parties to tackle the dreadful threat to this country has channelized protest into the CND. The 3,000 hard core of the march were made up mainly of people under twenty-five, in many cases under eighteen. Only about a quarter of the youthful marchers were politically conscious—and most of these were identified with Socialist groups. The majority had no politics more complicated than the conviction that nuclear threats were intolerable. Their placards bore inscriptions like YOUTH SAYS NO or WE WANT TO LIVE. The press made much of their songs, blue jeans, beards and eccentric hats. There is no doubt that the protest against the bomb has merged with a larger protest of British youth against the stuffiness and dullness of their parents' lives, against the tight-lipped hypocrisy and the unadulterated humbug which befog this island. For many, then, it was their first demonstration; quite a few came . . . from places not usually associated with protest movements of any sort.

These were largely middle-class youngsters: university and high school students, novice artists and musicians. . . . The emphasis on youth seemed to cut across many of the usual divisions—including thirty or forty young Tory marchers—and lots of young Liberals, and plenty of old ones; the Liberal party has in fact declared for unilateral British atomic disarmament.

The procession, on that first day, made an extraordinary impression as it wound through the flat and gentle Berkshire countryside. It was headed by a jazz group, the drummer in kilts. Silence was the word as we passed the atomic-weapons center, stared at by blue-uniformed guards and their dogs. The combination of pale blue sky, thick white clouds, jazz rhythms, the clump of thousands of marching feet, and the architecture of death beside us was incongruous—so incongruous that it seemed to fit our time exactly. Above our heads: innumerable banners, slogans and the semaphore signal of CND carried on something that resembled a giant lollipop. The banners identified the contingents: combined universities, the local CND groups, Quakers, the youth committees. The slogans were often graphic: one pictured a home-made but appropriately repulsive dinosaur: TOO MUCH ARMOR, TOO LITTLE BRAIN: HE DIED. Leaflet distributers were out on either flank, pausing to argue with those who challenged them. Motor scooters and motorcycles flying the CND flag went up and down alongside, and we had our own autocade, which pulled up at stops to disgorge supplies of food and the inevitable tea. The jazz band and a West Indian steel band supplied music.

There were foreign contingents, a big one from Germany, another from Sweden, lots of Asian and African students—and an occasional U.S.A. on a semaphore bobbing above a crew cut. A number of baby carriages were in evidence. That night, and the next two, thousands were bedded down in sleeping bags on school, church or city-hall floors. . . .

On the fourth and final day, the composition of the march altered. The trade unionists now came on, there were many more families, hundreds marched behind a Methodist bishop, City men [businessmen from the financial center of London] with furled umbrellas appeared, a good many stage, screen and TV personnel fell in, and London's *literati* abandoned their typewriters for the day. My own contingent, Universities and Left Review, had marched from Aldermaston with about 150; we entered Trafalgar Square with some 600. The sensation of the day, apart from the dramatic increase in our numbers, was the appearance on the platform of the president of the Trades Union Congress, Robert Willis. (The most influential trade unionist in Britain, Frank Cousins, joined the demonstration as well.) Willis said that he hoped and expected that if the march were needed next year, half the participants would be unionists. . . .

So the march from Aldermaston was a success, and a surprising one. . . . Not alone the fact that the marchers cared, but the quality of their concern—an affirmation of the simple value of human life itself—had an impact. It isn't accidental, perhaps, that the only consistently hostile response we met on the march came from two groups, at either end of the age and status scale. The "Teddy Boys," the working-class juveniles consumed by resentment at their lack of opportunities in the "opportunity state," were full of sneers. And the ex-officer types . . . were choleric. Each of these groups, of course, has come to a psychological dead end; neither can accept new experience. . . .

Some people here are looking across the ocean. Fifteen thousand marchers in London could be matched only by fifty thousand in Washington. It may be objected that there are no nuclear-protest marches in Moscow. (The British Communist party . . . at first boycotted CND because its leaders persisted in saying this; they've now given the campaign their support—with the reservation that criticism of the U.S.S.R. is unsporting.) But it is difficult to see how the Soviet people can be induced to take the risks of freedom if those to whom freedom is given do not use it to protest on behalf of all mankind. The Aldermaston march was a step—a step fifty-three miles long—in the right direction.

THE DEEPER MEANING OF BRITISH NEUTRALISM [2]

Young people of the Campaign for Nuclear Disarmament marching defiantly and gaily on pilgrimages to nuclear research centers or United States air bases, hot-eyed orators expounding "unilateralism" in frowsty village halls, militants of the extreme Left shouting down Hugh Gaitskell at Labour party meetings—all are manifestations of the neutralist movement in Britain. With its anti-Americanism, its pacifism, its appeal to youth's crusading spirit, its isolationism and its contribution to the policy objectives of the Soviet Union, the neutralist movement is perhaps the most significant phenomenon of postwar British political history.

It is impossible to say how far the movement will go. Experienced politicians like Prime Minister Macmillan believe that

[2] From article by Drew Middleton, chief of the London bureau of the New York *Times*. New York *Times Magazine*. p. 12+. D. 11, '60. Reprinted by permission.

it is only a "froth"—that the British are "essentially sound at heart." The Oxford undergraduates who, in the thirties, pledged themselves not to fight "for King and country" and who, not long after, were killed fighting Germans are cited as proof that "if a test comes" Britons will "stand by the Crown, the Church and the laws and show the old lion still has his claws."

This hopeful forecast may overlook the instinctive understanding that should nuclear war come most Britons—and Americans, Germans, Frenchmen and Russians—will have no choice but to die. The contemporary world, the neutralists say, is one wherein truth and justice cannot be attained by war because no one would remain to enjoy them after a war.

The neutralist movement has not yet reached its apogee. A general election today would result in a rout of the neutralists, but there is no certainty that five years hence they might not win a general election fought in a worsening international atmosphere that would focus popular attention on the extreme vulnerability of this island.

The most significant advance of the neutralist movement occurred at the annual Labour party conference at Scarborough in October [1960]. [This conference and its implications for Labour party unity are discussed in "England's Labour Party," in Section II, above.] The conference approved a resolution imposing a policy of unilateral nuclear disarmament on the party.

The resolution also rejected any defense policy based on the threat of the use of strategic or tactical nuclear weapons, called for an end to the use of British bases for aircraft carrying nuclear weapons and opposed the establishment of missile bases in the United Kingdom. The effect of this and other resolutions, if carried out by a Labour government, would be to take the United Kingdom out of NATO.

This neutralist victory has had no immediate effect upon British policy. But, with Hugh Gaitskell, the Labour party leader and a firm supporter of the Atlantic alliance, fighting to reverse the resolution, it has widened the gap within the Labour party to a point where it may be irreparable. And it has disclosed the strength of the neutralists in British politics, indicating that the clamor of the Campaign for Nuclear Disarmament has moved hard-headed politicians of the Left to support its views.

The strength of neutralism was demonstrated again early in November when Prime Minister Macmillan announced an agreement with the United States to provide anchorage for United States ballistic-missile submarines in the Holy Loch off Scotland's Firth of Clyde. The announcement produced an outburst of indignation in Parliament, in the country and in the press of quite unusual bitterness. Many people, like Lord Beaverbrook, who have no sympathy with Soviet policies opposed the Holy Loch anchorage on the grounds of Britain's independence of the United States. Anti-Americanism is inextricably linked with neutralism, and it has been growing in this country, as demonstrated most recently by the uproar over the Ford Company's offer to buy up the outstanding stock in its British subsidiary.

Neutralism feeds also on many Britons' understandable but lamentable distrust and hatred of Germany. This has been exacerbated by every step taken to strengthen the West German military position. In fact, neutralism first emerged as a force in postwar British politics when German rearmament was at issue seven years ago. The establishment of nuclear power for NATO, to which West Germany belongs, inevitably would strengthen the neutralists.

The Campaign for Nuclear Disarmament is the strongest arm of the neutralist movement. The original campaigners included men like Bertrand Russell, Canon Lewis J. Collins of St. Paul's, Ian Mikardo and Michael Foot of Labour's left wing, J. B. Priestley and an important section of the intelligentsia. Support came at once from the radical left wing of the Labour party, a small but very vocal minority. The campaign also attracted from the outset a high proportion of a potentially important political group in Britain. This comprises teachers, scientists and technical workers who are graduates of the minor "red brick" universities [the newer universities without the status of Oxford and Cambridge]. Well educated, hungry for advancement, working for low wages, they feel themselves outsiders in the complacent, prosperous, materialist Britain of today.

But the campaign got its real impetus from youth. As young people flocked to it, the movement became more dynamic, transforming itself from a somewhat narrowly based organization into something infinitely more important. "For thousands of young people, unilateral nuclear disarmament is the only cause that really matters," the [Manchester] *Guardian* has commented. "They see it as a moral crusade and even more as an obvious necessity for personal survival."

As the campaign progressed, staging impressive demonstrations in London and the provinces, the Communist party promoted the cause of neutralism in key trade unions. But neither the Campaign for Nuclear Disarmament nor the Communists would have progressed so rapidly had they not been exploiting sentiments deeply embedded in British society.

Pacifism, for instance, is strong in the Nonconformist North and in Wales. A strain of pacifism is apparent in British political history from the Boer War onward. There also are many people of all political creeds who, fearful of Britain's vulnerability in a nuclear war, distrust military control, especially non-British military control, of nuclear weapons based here.

But the basic motivation underlying this movement is far deeper. No explanation of British neutralism makes sense unless it is understood that the British have never been completely internationalist in their attitude.

Circumstances have forced the British people into deep involvement in world affairs. But isolationism, the instinct to withdraw into their island shell, is as much a part of the British ethos as what the Victorians and Edwardians called the imperial spirit.

Periodically Britons have tried to turn inward, away from the world and their allies. . . . Only a quarter of a century ago, Stanley Baldwin, a "Little Englander" [opposed to territorial expansion of the British Empire] who was bored by foreign affairs, ruled from Downing Street. His successor, Neville

Chamberlain, once publicly deplored the possibility that Britain might have to fight for Czechoslovakia, which he termed a far-off country of whose people Britons knew little.

Historically, of course, the pull of the world outside, the nation's vital overseas interests, proved stronger. But the yearning for a horizon bounded by the island's coasts has always remained. Its concomitant is neutralism.

The psychological appeal of neutralism is strong for a variety of reasons. Fear exists, but it does not seem to be a particularly personal fear. Rather, it is that nuclear war will mean the final end of the long British history with all its disasters and triumphs.

The British do not expect that this country could emerge as a viable society from nuclear attack. This estimate is held both by the Government—convinced of the deterrent power of nuclear weapons—and by the Campaign for Nuclear Disarmament. After all, it does not require a particularly lively imagination to understand what would have happened to London and Britain if the German rockets that fell on this island between September 1944 and early 1945 had been armed with nuclear warheads.

Oddly, national pride, a desire for national achievement, motivates many unilateralists. "If we can take Britain out of the arms race," a young student from Reading University said, "we will have given an example to the world, one that you Americans don't dare give."

For Britain to take the first step, to exercise its "moral influence," is terribly important to the campaigners for nuclear disarmament. They sincerely believe the present disarmament deadlock is more likely to be broken if Britain abandons her nuclear arms, that such an action would move public opinion in the United States, France and even the Soviet Union to press for nuclear disarmament. . . .

Moreover, the movement's crusading aspect harmonizes with the strong evangelical spirit that has run through British politics from Cromwell to Cripps and that has often been at odds with imperialism. "The basis of neutrality is not indifference; it is not self-interest," said Woodrow Wilson in 1915. "The basis of neutrality is sympathy for mankind." This is a note that one hears echoed in the speeches of the neutralists in Britain.

There is also a less inspirational side to neutralism. From a material standpoint, more British people are living well today than ever before in the country's history. Appeals to get out of the arms race—and cut taxes—to forget about NATO—and other expensive responsibilities—have an impact upon people who, in Prime Minister Macmillan's phrase, have "never had it so good" and would like to have it better. This impact, it should be noted, is greatest among that section of the population, the prosperous working class and new middle class, that would not be affected by the crusading appeal of the Campaign for Nuclear Disarmament or by left-wing oratory.

Neutralism and unilateralism, in effect, if not in original intent, are anti-American. They are one side of a struggle that has gone on since the war in Britons' minds—a struggle that thus far has gone in favor of those who wish to cleave to an alliance that has won two wars and kept Western Europe free since 1945.

Every national leader since Winston Churchill has supported this alliance. So have all responsible newspapers. The majority of Britons over forty is conscious of what the alliance has meant to survival and victory in the past and, although these people may not be outspokenly grateful, they would regard a rupture of the alliance as a national calamity.

Yet the weight of indifference or hostility to the United States and the alliance should not be underestimated. The popular picture of America is as alarming as it is false. Many in this country picture the United States as a grossly materialist nation whose policies are influenced by aggressive nationalism at best, or by power-mad militarists at worst. The scars left on many Britons of the conservative middle and upper classes by American intervention in the Suez adventure have never really healed, despite four years of effort by Mr. Macmillan. Anti-Americanism is most vocal on the Left, but it is latent in the Center and strong—and often outspoken—on the Right.

Exaggerated anti-Americanism on the Left should not blind Americans, however, to the way in which off-the-cuff remarks in Washington about military action worry Britons. Anything suggesting trigger-happy militarists in the Pentagon sounds alarm bells in British minds. It is worth remembering that to many here "the Pentagon" and "the Kremlin" are equated as citadels of power, either of which might give the signal for a final holocaust for this island.

The decline of British power in relation to that of the United States and the Soviet Union understandably has brought British nationalism into the open. One of its faces is the unilateralists' demand that "Britain take the lead." . . .

The desire for independence from the colossi of Washington and Moscow, whether it takes the form of neutralism in Britain or chauvinistic nationalism in France, is undoubtedly a force in the world's attitude toward the United States and the Soviet Union.

The governments of Western Europe, particularly, have been captives of the cold war for nearly fifteen years. They are committed to the policies of the United States. But one of the strongest emotional factors behind the appeal to Europeans of a United Europe is that its organization would replace the leadership of an alien United States with a European supranational government, economically powerful and armed to a point where it could talk on a basis of equality with the giants of East and West.

United Europe, either through the European Economic Community the [Common Market] or some other organization, is one means of escaping—or at least avoiding—United States hegemony in the affairs of the West. Neutralism as it is pursued in Britain is another means to this end.

These trends, observable among the oldest and most stable of America's allies, are more pronounced farther afield. Pan-Africanism has as one of its objectives the avoidance of political or military ties with either West or East. To the new men coming to the top in Britain's remaining African possessions, there is no contradiction in a situation wherein their countries receive economic and technical aid from both sides, and yet remain neutral.

Such neutralism has a different basis from that in Britain. There is no immediate military involvement for Nigeria or Nyasaland in the cold war. But the desire to remove their countries from a world political conflict that might suddenly explode into nuclear war is common to neutralists everywhere.

Although Britain's material power has declined rapidly in relation to the United States and the U.S.S.R., she has maintained considerable influence around the world, possibly as a holdover from the nineteenth century, when a large part of the world was run from London, possibly because the British—with three hundred years of parliamentary democracy behind them—still have political stature among the emerging nations.

This influence is not exerted solely through the Government. Indeed, many of those around the world who look to Britain for political inspiration look to the Left—in fact, to that section of the Left that leads the fight for unilateralism and neutralism.

This is the final importance of the growth of neutralism in Britain. Whether it succeeds or fails in changing the policies of future British governments, it cannot help but exert considerable influence upon the new nations of Africa and Asia. Indeed, if successful, it would have considerable influence upon Western Europe as well.

THE NON-NUCLEAR CLUB [3]

Properly to understand the "non-nuclear club" debate in Britain, one has to recognize the political as well as the military complications. It was a Labour Government which vigorously promoted the North Atlantic Treaty Organization in 1949. Then the United States had the monopoly of the atomic bomb. The European NATO members were to provide the conventional fighting forces which would discourage the Russians from ambling across Europe, but if they felt tempted to do so, they would have to reckon with the paramount weapon, delivered

[3] From article by Ritchie Calder, British author and scientist. *Bulletin of the Atomic Scientists*. 16:123-6. Ap. '60. Reprinted by permission.

within the Soviet Union by American bombers. But it was also the Labour Government which decided that Britain should have its own bomb. (One does not recall that the United States was wildly enthusiastic about this supplemental nuclear help.) But, by the time Britain had tested her A-bomb in 1952, Russia had fired hers and was stockpiling. Thus Britain found herself inviting attack on two counts—as the advanced base for the American bombers, which she had received on her territory, and as the independent maker and potential user of atom bombs. And the United States found herself with an ally capable of independent nuclear initiative. All this happened under a Labour Government and, with the rearmament of Germany which it accepted under NATO dispensation, accounts for present disagreements, aggravated rather than resolved by the non-nuclear club arguments.

There was, however, no apparent reluctance on the part of the Conservative Government to accept the commitments. Indeed, Sir Winston Churchill impishly expressed his gratified surprise at finding himself in possession of atomic weapons. His government went ahead and produced the H-bomb and a supporting missile program. But the stresses imposed on NATO by the introduction of the atomic weapons were already obvious. Member states, for many reasons, were "dragging their feet" in the provision of manpower and conventional weapons. It became the more imperative that Germany should be rearmed and that the missing battalions should be replaced by disposition of "tactical nuclear weapons."

In Britain, the costs of maintaining a standing National Service army and a nuclear weapons program mounted to proportions which would make any government unpopular, but there were other contradictions in British military policy. In fact . . . policy was nonexistent. The Defense White Paper of 1957 was undefensive and indefensible. It based its reliance on guided missiles and, in order to pay for them, proceeded to liquidate historic British regiments. The Defense Minister, Mr. Duncan Sandys, committed himself to the following statement in Australia: "We have taken a very bold step in deciding not to do the impossible. We decided not to defend the whole country, but to defend only our bomber bases. I must pay tribute to the people of Great Britain for the readiness with which they have accepted these harsh, inescapable facts."

This was the first that the British people knew of the heroic, self-sacrificial role for which they had been cast.

Somehow, this had to be reconciled to NATO and, in 1958, it was affirmed that any major act of aggression by the Russians, even with conventional weapons, would be countered by British nuclear weapons. Brave words! But since the same Minister had already made it plain that any initiation of nuclear war by Britain would mean the total destruction of the country and its people, this statement was cynically received by those who might have reason to fear Russian military intentions. It would simply mean that Britain would never define "major aggression," since to do so would be an act of suicide.

This policy had the political value of reducing the defense budget by £200 million ($560 million) and of securing the end of National Service in 1960. But it also disrupted NATO planning for an adequate land strength in Europe and forced NATO to rely more and more on tactical nuclear weapons, at a time when the feasibility of using such weapons was being hotly disputed.

In Britain, where serving officers (unless they are field marshals!) are not supposed to make policy utterances, internecine, interservice squabbles are conducted behind locked doors and on "the old school tie" principle. But no one could have any doubts of the violent disagreements. Indeed, on a military doctrine dictated by political expediency, the Chiefs of Staff were confronted with what Blackett [Professor P. M. S. Blackett, a Nobel Laureate and strong advocate of the non-nuclear club] has called "defeat by syllogism":

"The enemy attacks with conventional forces; we reply with atomic bombs on his cities. If his cities are attacked, the enemy will attack ours. If a country has no effective civil defense against atomic bombs, and its cities are attacked it will be defeated. None of our cities has any civil defense." *Ergo. . . .*

Ordinary people, in Britain or Europe, may find it difficult to grasp orders of magnitude, or sometimes, to distinguish between kilotons and megatons, but the adult population, which survived the last war, can grasp the fact that one warhead, minimized as "tactical," could be equal, in destructive power, to the raid which "coventrated" Coventry, or perhaps a thousand-bomber raid on Cologne. They can add what they know about radiation hazards, and for them, in the front line, a limited nuclear war is too unlimited. They might not have followed the refinements of the "strategical" and "tactical" arguments, . . . but even two years ago, what they sensed or knew packed them into the biggest halls in the country and pushed them on the roads, in what is admitted to be the most powerful nonparty political movement since the war—the Campaign for Nuclear Disarmament.

Non-Nuclear Club Proposed

At that stage . . . [in 1958], the Campaign, apart from the strong emotions which it released or generated, marked a new phase. It declared itself for "unilateral disarmament," demanding that Britain should take the lead in renouncing the testing, the making, the possessing or using of nuclear weapons, and rejecting guided missile sites and bomber bases. Its aim, "unilateralism," was at variance with all parties, including the Communists, and while ostensibly, its attacks were directed against the Government, its pressures were mainly upon, and through, the Labour party as the alternative government. This is relevant to the origins of the non-nuclear club.

Peers, sympathetic to the Campaign, promoted a debate in the House of Lords, in February . . . [1959]. Such matters are conducted with decorum in Their Lordships' House and, to accommodate party Peers and avoid collisions with the party whips, speeches were tempered and compromises reached. Most speakers were dutifully mindful of Britain's commitments to NATO. Out of that debate came, from a Labour Peer, the suggestion of a "non-nuclear club," with Britain taking the initiative and being prepared to renounce her own weapons as an inducement to other countries to join. . . .

In April 1959 we had Secretary of State Herter's statement: "I cannot conceive any President engaging in an all-out nuclear war, unless we are in danger of all-out nuclear destruction ourselves." This was interpreted in Europe as meaning that America was relying . . . on the threat of nuclear saturation reprisals to deter Russia from direct attack on the United States. This was taken to mean that an "incident" in Europe would not, as in the original intention of NATO, invoke the strategical bomb in support of European allies. This led to the logic . . . that if there were national, or West European nuclear weapons, and they were employed, they would inevitably "force the hand" of the United States.

Thus it became plain that, as more and more countries developed the capacity to make bombs, Europe, and indeed the whole world, would be littered with nuclear booby-traps which would detonate a nuclear war and, willy-nilly, involve the United States and Russia. As *Daedalus,* the journal of the American Academy of Arts and Sciences, has pointed out, at least twelve countries are already capable of doing so—Belgium, China, Canada, Czechoslovakia, France, East Germany, West Germany, India, Italy, Japan, Sweden, and Switzerland. Within five years, another fourteen countries may be capable of starting atomic weapons. . . .

The debate continues. And, regardless of parties or of NATO, the Campaign for Nuclear Disarmament goes on arguing with its marching feet.

BRITISH STILL HOPE FOR SUMMIT [4]

When Mallory was asked why he wanted to climb Everest, he replied: "Because it's there." Prime Minister Macmillan's renewed advocacy of a summit conference owes something to this attitude. The summit is there.

[4] From "British Still Hope for 1961 Summit," by Drew Middleton, chief of the London bureau of the New York *Times*. New York *Times News of the Week in Review.* p E7. O. 23, '60. Reprinted by permission.

When Mr. Macmillan told the Conservative party that negotiations between East and West on Berlin and Germany would
have to be resumed, he was stating what is to him obvious.
Germany, Berlin, disarmament are important, inherently dangerous issues that must be discussed somewhere seriously. It is better in the British view to keep the Russians talking with some
hope of negotiation than to relapse into a hostile silence broken
only by blasts from the propaganda batteries.

Mr. Macmillan's frank advocacy of a summit—"I'm all for
it"—has worried a great many people in Europe who do not
understand or who do not want to understand the nuances of
British policy toward the Soviet Union. They regard that policy
as contradictory and superficially at least, this is so.

For the British Government, most recently through the Prime
Minister and his new Foreign Secretary, the Earl of Home,
have made it clear that Britain stands firmly with the West,
that she has no intention of giving in anywhere to Soviet pressure.
But at the same time Mr. Macmillan makes it clear that he
wants to resume high-level talks with Premier Khrushchev.

The alarm aroused by this seeming contradiction owes something to the uneasiness felt by many on the basis of half-
remembered tales of Munich. The Prime Minister thus began
his second attempt to conquer a summit in an unfavorable if
not hostile atmosphere.

Immediate opposition was generated, as it was in 1959, in
West Germany. Dr. Adenauer was not invited to attend the
last summit and it is doubtful if he would attend a new one.

Recently he told Western diplomats in Bonn that Mr.
Khrushchev's grotesque behavior at the United Nations was
what they should expect in any summit negotiation and that
there was no more hope of holding serious, substantive talks
with him than there would be of discussing Kant with a baboon.

Dr. Adenauer's view is that it is best to leave Berlin alone,
that the situation there is all right and that any negotiations
on it would weaken the Western position. Dr. Adenauer's
present opposition to a summit meeting is as strong as was his
objection a year ago.

Of the three Western participants in the summit meeting, President de Gaulle was the least enthusiastic. But his reluctance of a year ago to go to the summit probably has been strengthened this year by problems that have suddenly beclouded the reign of a man the *Economist* calls Charles the Tall.

The Algerian problem has become as disruptive and emotional a problem to Gaullist France as Ireland was to Edwardian England. At the same time President de Gaulle's projects to make France an independent nuclear power and Europe a union of fatherlands are under severe attack, the first at home and the second abroad.

We are left with only the British Government solidly behind a renewal of summit talks. One reason for London's persistence, despite last spring's fiasco and the fantastic futility of the East-West confrontation at the General Assembly, is that the [British] Government . . . recognizes the possibility of an international situation that will force a summit meeting upon the West.

On the optimistic side, there is hope, certainly not considered bright in London at the moment, that enough headway will be made toward disarmament at the lower level to warrant high-level negotiation. . . .

The British fear the West might be dragged to a conference table by the logic of events were the Soviet Union to start peace talks with East Germany or to prompt the East Germans to begin those unidentifiably hostile acts against West Berlin's communications that would in time sap its economic vitality.

Preparation Sought

These are the kinds of situations that might force a summit conference on the West, in the British view. The obvious alternative, to Mr. Macmillan and his advisers, is to start a methodical, thorough preparation now for a summit conference to be held before the situation deteriorates and indeed, to prevent its deterioration.

Will such reasoning induce General de Gaulle to accept summit talks? Perhaps not. But in assessing the forces operating for and against a conference, the British point to a reason directly connected with President de Gaulle's preoccupation with Algeria.

Although ebulliently admiring the Algerian representatives at the United Nations, Mr. Khrushchev has avoided outright diplomatic and military support of the rebels. The impression . . . [in Britain] is that he will continue to do so while there is a prospect of a meeting at the summit. In the end this may weigh more heavily with President de Gaulle than any situation favorable or unfavorable, concerning Berlin or disarmament.

Perhaps the most important factor in moving Mr. Macmillan toward another summit was his talks with Mr. Khrushchev in New York. From these it was concluded that the Soviet Premier was ready to attend a summit conference in the spring, that he felt it would be futile to hold a meeting before the new United States Administration was firmly in the saddle, and that he had no intention at present of bringing continuous and violent pressure to bear on West Berlin or blockading it while there was a reasonable chance that East and West could discuss Berlin's future before next summer [1961].

No Real Alternative

A summit conference, the British readily agree, is not to everyone's taste. But they regard it as far more attractive than the final suggestion thrown out by Mr. Khrushchev to Mr. Macmillan.

The Soviet Premier proposed a peace conference of all states at war with Germany between 1939 and 1945. The object would be to sign peace treaties with East and West Germany.

These treaties would end the state of war and the occupation status of the Western forces in West Berlin, which rests on their rights as conquerors. This would be a larger, more complex diplomatic challenge than any summit conference and one that could do the Western cause in Europe a great deal of damage.

PROSPECTS OF MANKIND [5]

Mrs. Roosevelt. Lord Russell, you have been taking a leading part in the debate about what Britain should do in regard to nuclear armament. We would be much interested to hear what you really think British policy should be?

Lord Russell. I think myself that Britain should give up not only the personal possession and manufacture of nuclear weapons, but all reliance on nuclear weapons for her own defense. I should like to see Britain become a neutral in the cold war for a variety of reasons which I dare say we shall be able to go into soon.

Hugh Gaitskell. For my part, I disagree very much with what Lord Russell said at the end of his remarks. I do not think it would be at all wise for us to give up the NATO alliance. Indeed, I think this would be profoundly dangerous to peace and freedom. It would either mean the breakup of the alliance, which would leave the whole of Western Europe open to Soviet pressure or threats, or it might continue in a different form, in which case probably the role of Germany would be much stronger and we should have lost all our influence upon American policy; and the consequence would be a sharpening of the conflict between East and West.

Lord Boothby. On this point I am on Hugh Gaitskell's side. It would be a great mistake for us to get out of NATO, although I think that NATO itself as an alliance leaves much to be desired and requires a radical revision of the whole of its political structure. But we must be in it. At the same time I also think we should not have an independent nuclear weapon of our own. If NATO is to be an effective and real alliance then there should be one final deterrent for the alliance as a whole, and that should be under the ultimate control and authority of the United States.

[5] From a discussion of the defense policy of Britain, broadcast by the British Broadcasting Corporation. Participants were Eleanor Roosevelt; Bertrand Russell, eminent mathematician, philosopher, and author; the Right Hon. Hugh Gaitskell, leader of the Labour party in England; Lord Boothby, member of the House of Lords; and Robert McKenzie, teacher at the London School of Economics, and writer. *Listener.* 114:543-8. O. 6, '60. Reprinted by permission.

Mrs. Roosevelt. That puts a good deal of responsibility on the United States. You advocate, Lord Russell, complete disarmament for Great Britain; do you also advocate that for other countries?

Lord Russell. I didn't say complete disarmament—I said complete lack of nuclear weapons. I do not advocate it for the United States. Short of an agreement with Russia—I think that the United States Government ought to do all it can to get a disarmament agreement with Russia—I am not advocating unilateral renunciation of nuclear weapons by the United States.

Robert McKenzie. You are not in that sense, then, Lord Russell, a pacifist? You do not advocate giving up all weapons by the Western countries?

Lord Russell. I have never been a complete pacifist at any time. During the First World War, which I opposed, I explained that there have been wars that I would have supported —and I supported the Second World War completely.

Robert McKenzie. Then you would argue that there is a rational case for Britain alone giving up, or the countries of Western Europe giving up, nuclear arms but not conventional arms? Could you give us the basic argument behind this claim?

Lord Russell. Yes—and the argument is the same for all the satellites of the United States. It was first developed by a perfectly orthodox American, Herman Kahn, before the U-2 incident. He pointed out that the Soviets could, if they chose, obliterate any one of the satellites of the United States, and that if they did so, in spite of obligations under NATO, it was likely that the United States would not go to war. He did not say this as a criticism of the United States, and no more do I. But let us suppose, for the sake of argument, that Britain has been completely wiped out so that we are all dead—which can be done in an hour quite easily. Let us suppose that has happened through a Russian attack. Then the President of the United States has to say: "Shall I, as a perfectly futile vengeance, decide that all the rest of the people in the world should die? What good would that do to anybody?" If the President at the moment happened to be a rational man—which is a not impossible supposition—then he would say: "No," in spite of NATO. "It's no use. They're dead. I can't help those corpses." That was said in this article before the U-2 incident. After the U-2 incident Khrushchev and Malinovsky proclaimed definitely that if any country allowed its territory to be used by the United States in ways that Russia thought offensive that country would be obliterated, wiped out—there would be nothing left of it, they said. I see no reason to suppose that that was an empty boast; I think it is very likely true. I think they could obliterate us completely without causing a general nuclear war. If they did cause a general nuclear war the argument would be still stronger.

Western Satellites?

Mrs. Roosevelt. But Lord Russell, it sounds very odd to me to have you talk about Western European countries as satellites of the United States. My understanding of a satellite, in the Eastern Hemisphere, is quite different from the feeling I would have about any of the Western countries who are now more or less closely allied with the United States. Your argument is that an American President, who was a rational man, would not, of course, come to the help of people who were wiped out. There is not much you can do for people once they are dead. But there would still be the consideration that you would be under Russian domination unless you did something to show that you were not going to let the Soviet Union wipe out one country after another. And without question I think it would lead to a third World War. I agree that such a war seems a very terrible thing because I don't see how we could save ourselves from being completely obliterated. On the other hand the idea that a country being wiped out would make the United States think it had to accept that and do nothing seems to me totally impossible, because you would then have capitulated to the power of Russia.

Lord Boothby. May I ask one point of Lord Russell? He admitted in what he said that it was conceivable that this country could be wiped out by Russia in an hour, and that I entirely agree to. What puzzles me about his attitude is that I should have thought it was less likely to happen if we were known to be in alliance with the United States and that American retaliatory power would definitely be used if that happened. Walter Lippmann has pointed out again and again that the only agreements that the Russians have kept have been geographical agreements, which laid down a line over which they could not go. They have never kept ideological agreements about democracy or anything like that, but on balance they have kept military and geographical agreements which fixed a line. I would rather be on our side of that line than in a nebulous, neutralist position; the risk of a general conflagration and certainly the risk of this country being wiped out would be much less.

Lord Russell. As to the word "satellite," I don't care two-pence—you can alter it and say merely allies of the United States. But so long as our territory is used by American military forces, as it is at present, and as it must be under NATO, so long the Russians have a motive for attacking us. It would be a most appalling thing if they did. I don't think we should be quite safe if we were out of NATO, but we should be safer, because they would not have the same motive. They do not, as a matter of fact, attack the uncommitted nations; I cannot think of any case where they have; and if we were uncommitted I do not believe they would attack us. I do not say the situation would be pleasant—I don't think it would—but I do think that the supposed protection that we derive from NATO is utterly illusory. The governments of the countries that are in NATO, the American government as well as the others, believe it is a real protection, but I think they deceive themselves: it is not, and we should be in less danger if we were out of it.

The Crux of the Matter

Hugh Gaitskell. It seems to me that the crux of this matter is what the Russians really are likely to do. What you are arguing, Lord Russell, is really this: you are saying, they're not going to believe that the Americans are going to strike even second, even if one of their allies is attacked, even presumably if they get to know that a rocket is on its way; they don't think it's going for them, and they keep clear. That is what you believe, because otherwise obviously your argument falls to the ground, doesn't it? Nevertheless you think the Russians are so frightened of Britain being an ally of America that they will all the same attack. This doesn't seem to me to add up at all.

Lord Russell. It adds up this way—that the Russians do not like Americans having bases near Russia.

Hugh Gaitskell. But you have already agreed that the Russians are not even frightened of the Americans hitting back. Why? Because, according to your argument, the Russians believe the Americans will be so frightened at themselves being obliterated. If that is the case, the Russians will certainly say to themselves there is no possible danger of America making the first strike. Therefore, in these circumstances, I cannot see the reason for the Russians taking this action, and I return to Boothby's point, if I may: what I cannot understand in your argument is that you really believe the Russians are more likely to attack us when, despite your argument, there must remain the possibility, the very real possibility, of retaliation; but, all the same, if we are neutral, and there is nobody to come to our aid to defend us at all, then the Russians will leave us alone. It simply doesn't seem to me to make sense. I mean, either the Russians are really very peacefully minded and not frightened at all, in which case they won't attack us, or if they are, on the contrary, ruthless "expansionists," then, if we are alone, I think we can say good-bye to freedom.

Lord Russell. May I ask you this one question: why do you think that the Russians are not attacking all the other uncommitted nations of the world?

Lord Boothby. I am old-fashioned maybe, but I really do believe in the balance of world power. I think NATO reestablished that when it was formed. On the whole it has been maintained for the last ten years, and I hope that it will be maintained indefinitely. I am not saying at what level it should be maintained—that is a subject for negotiation and agreement; I hope in future years it may be at a level less crippling to the economies of both the Communist world and the free world. But I do believe, genuinely and sincerely, that it is the balance of power that has prevented a war from breaking out in the last ten years, and that that, and that alone, will prevent a third World War.

The Uncommitted Countries

Hugh Gaitskell. I would just like to add this: you asked me the question, "Why don't they attack the uncommitted countries"—India for instance. I should say, first, because they are frightened of a nuclear war. I think they are perfectly sensible people; they are quite cautious people. I do not think the Russians are going to take enormous risks; but I do think that if they can achieve the expansion of communism without any cost to themselves, by mere threats, and they know there is virtually no risk of any retaliation, they will take advantage of that.

Lord Russell. Why do you think they have not done it in India?

Hugh Gaitskell. I think they have not done it in India, first of all because India is in fact a peculiarly well-defended country, geographically. It has a mountain range on one side, and it has sea on the other. I think they also don't know where this is going to end. After all, Pakistan is involved. Pakistan happens to be in the SEATO alliance. They don't know what America will do in those circumstances.

Robert McKenzie. It seems to me, while the weight of the panel is obviously against Lord Russell's argument, that this is a balance of risks. Lord Russell has said he is not an absolute pacifist, and therefore he does not belong to a category of people who would dispose of both the nuclear weapons and conventional weapons on principle. But he has argued on balance that the risk is less for Britain and Western Europe if it gets out of the NATO alliance and disposes of its own nuclear weapons.

Others in the panel—clearly a majority—have taken a contrary view: that the balance of risk is far greater on the other side. . . .

The Disarmament Question

Robert McKenzie. Whatever distinguished individuals may say about unilateral disarmament, we have apparently the possibility of one of the two major political parties in this country committing itself to unilateral disarmament. I think Mr. Gaitskell owes it to us to say how this prospect appears to be.

Hugh Gaitskell. What I will do is to try to make perfectly plain what the issues are here. As far as the executive committee, the leadership of the Labour party, and indeed of the Trades Union Congress is concerned, and the parliamentary Labour party by an overwhelming majority, this is our view. Namely, first, that of course we must put as absolutely top priority the strengthening of the United Nations and ultimately world government, as the only final solution of this problem. Secondly, that we must continue—and here I do not think there is any disagreement between any of us—to do everything in our power to achieve multilateral disarmament. I will come back to the Pentagon later. Thirdly, however, that the United Nations being what it is, with the veto, with the division of the world into two blocs, you cannot expect the Security Council to defend, or the United Nations to defend, any country that is attacked; and therefore because of that you have to have allies of your own. And we believe that NATO was formed for that reason, and has been a major force in preventing war, and that we should remain in NATO. On the other hand, we also say that so long as the Soviet Union possesses nuclear weapons, then the Western alliance somewhere should have them too. Then, we say on the other hand, that so long as the West has the power of retaliation, the deterrent theory applies, as far as we are concerned in Britain—that is a different issue.

I agree with Russell there, the question of what Britain does, and what the West does in the international field must be distinguished. Now we believe that the time has come for

Britain to give up the idea of having her own independent
nuclear deterrent. And that time, indeed, has been forced upon
us, so as to speak, by the decision of the Government. However,
in our view a right decision would be to abandon the Blue
Streak rocket [a missile project that was abandoned by the
Government]. To put it in another way, when you are discussing the whole immensely complicated field of rockets carrying
hydrogen bombs, we have to face the fact that America spends
on research and development in this field alone more than the
whole of our defense expenditure. In these circumstances we
think it is foolish to compete with her, and here I agree with
Boothby that we should leave the provision of the nuclear
deterrent to the United States, though remaining members of
NATO ourselves. On the bases question, this is our position:
it is not a matter of principle; but you either say to the Americans "No bases!" or you say to the Americans: "Take anything
you like, bring anything you like." Obviously, you must discuss
this on the basis of the merits. Now, we are against the Thor
missiles. That, as it happens, is not an American base because
the Thor missiles are manned by British troops. But we think
they are a peculiarly foolish and vulnerable weapon, a first-strike
weapon. They could be eliminated immediately, and we have
always been against them on those grounds. As far as the
bases are concerned, it is a matter of negotiation. But you could
not, in my opinion, remain in an alliance and refuse to do what
you believe to be militarily necessary for that alliance. . . .

American Bases in Britain

Lord Boothby. At the moment, the Strategic American Air
Command's front line bases are in this country. It seems likely
that if we are to be able effectively to deliver the deterrent
weapon, that must continue at least for some time to come. I
would be in agreement with you and admit that this is probably
only a temporary problem, covering the next two or three years
only. Ultimately, I suppose, we shall have these horrible Sputniks
floating round, each one loaded with an atomic bomb which can

be ordered home on a particular base. One of them might fall down by accident, and that would be most unfortunate for all concerned. But for the next three or four years, to come back to my balance of power, to match the missile strength of the Russians we might have the front line of SAC here in this country. Would you agree that that is necessary? I think it is.

Hugh Gaitskell. I think it probably is, and I said earlier on, if it is militarily necessary, in the interests of the alliance, we could not, in my opinion, refuse it. . . .

Lord Russell. . . . The Labour party has been losing in recent years because it did not stand for anything much, and I think that the young, especially, of whom I know a great many, have a feeling that it would be rather nice to be allowed to grow up, and that if the present policies of the world continue they will have very little chance of reaching maturity before they are dead. That feeling is really very widespread, and the party that appealed to it would, I think, before long sweep the country. That is my deliberate opinion, based upon an astonishing growth of that way of looking at things.

Hugh Gaitskell. I can only say that I do not agree with that. But in any event this is an issue of such profound importance that I do not think we should make up our minds on it according to whether we think this young person or that is moving this way or that. If I think, as I do, that the policy you are advocating is profoundly dangerous, then I am going to oppose it.

Dangerous Policies

Lord Russell. Every policy is dangerous, but I think your policy is even more dangerous; it is as dangerous, with respect, as the policy you advocated before the last war, which was one of appeasement with Hitler.

Robert McKenzie. I want Boothby to say, very briefly, how the official Government position, the Government he used to support before he became an Independent, differs from the official position which the Labour party still holds.

Lord Boothby. From a purely practical point of view, the Government's position does not greatly differ from Gaitskell's position. They do not make it clear what they want. They have given up, as Gaitskell said, the Blue Streak weapon, and at the moment we are not a nuclear power. I would be very reluctant to see us ever become a nuclear power again. I want to get right in with the United States. Admittedly it throws, as Mrs. Roosevelt has said, a grave responsibility on the United States, but as a great power, and the only great power in the Western alliance, that is a responsibility they have got to accept. We accepted it, after all, in the nineteenth century: it was British sea power that really kept the peace of the world. I believe in the twentieth century it is American nuclear power that is going to keep the peace of the world, and we should accept that. I would give all the scientific advice, assistance, bases, to the Americans that they require. But I would not attempt to set ourselves up as an independent nuclear power as de Gaulle wants to do with France, for one simple reason amongst others—we simply have not got enough money to do it. I think in practice, if not in theory, that is the Government's position. The great thing about the Conservatives is—and that is why they are always elected in this country—they do not have theories; they do not have these policies that Lord Russell advocates; they do not have anything, except they do go on to do from their point of view what seems to be best at any given moment; and, if anything, they are doing a bit better than they were at the last election. They won the election. It is this awful pinning yourselves down to specific, concrete idealistic policies, which probably will never be carried out, that is the misfortune of the Labour party. And if a government does not need to do this, why the opposition should think it necessary to do so is beyond my comprehension.

The Greatest Misfortune?

Mrs. Roosevelt. . . . You said that we would recognize that a nuclear war was the greatest misfortune that could happen, and that in preference to that, either side winning would be better. . . .

I think most people in the United States . . . would say: "If we have to be dominated by the Soviet Union we would rather be wiped out." I think that is the majority opinion in the U.S.A.

Lord Russell. The Soviet Union could also be wiped out: the thing you have got to face is, would you rather have no human beings at all existing, or have world-wide dominion of the Soviet government?

Hugh Gaitskell. Oh no, with great respect, this is not the question; this is the whole point really. We do not believe that is the alternative. We believe it is possible to have both freedom and peace so long as we retain, in the West, the nuclear deterrent. And this is the main difference.

Lord Russell. You misunderstood what I meant. I was simply putting this alternative: if you had to choose between there being no human beings and there being a universal dominion of the Soviets, which would you choose?

Hugh Gaitskell. I think the questions we can discuss are the real questions—and not the hypothetical question.

Lord Boothby. Lord Russell has put a hypothetical question which I would rather like to answer. He has not always in his writings in the past taken that high an opinion of human beings as such. He is now giving them tremendous importance. In the last fifty years there have been moments when I was not at all sure in my own mind that it would not be better if the whole thing packed up because they are behaving like lunatics most of the time, and the 1939-1945 war was a piece of raging, hideous lunacy, and I should not like to see it repeated. There-fore, I would like to ask this hypothetical question straight, so as to answer it. I would much rather see the whole thing blown up than turned into a Communist world. If that was the alterna-tive I would say, let's go on somewhere else, and see if we can't do better there than we can here. But those of us who think as, basically, Gaitskell and myself and Mrs. Roosevelt think, are trying to stop that happening: you think one course is more dangerous, we think the other one is safer; but our object, after all, is to save the human race—although I doubt sometimes myself if it deserves it.

Robert McKenzie. In other words, we have come back to the point that it is a balance of risks. . . .

Lord Russell. . . . What I think would remove the risk would be a genuine belief on the part of governments that that was a thing to face.

Mrs. Roosevelt. I cannot speak for our present Administration—I do not happen to be a Republican and I do not happen to be on the inside of information—but when you say you cannot agree with Pentagon policies I think sometimes you have to balance what you hear about the influence on administration of the Army, which is practically what the Pentagon means, and the general feeling of the country. I would say that the people of our country would not be in agreement if the policy was one of aggression. You say that the general opinion is that the United States is in favor of war: I would say the United States was opposed to war. At the present time a certain number of us, and powerful people, believe that this balance of military power must be kept. I am hopeful that we are going to find ways, and one of the things that worries me is that we do not think more about the fact of how we move towards mutual total disarmament because, in the end, that is the only thing for us all. I think much thought everywhere should be brought to bear on even the smallest first move that can be made; I would like to see any little step forward. That is the attitude of the American people, and I am willing to acknowledge that the Pentagon—perhaps naturally, being military people—have more military ideas than I have, for instance, more than some other people. But I cannot help believing that the real difficulty is not going to be solved by neutralism. It is possible that it will be solved better through thinking and influence, through participation of all the group in Western Europe thinking how they can most safely take each step which brings us into some kind of agreement with the Soviet Union. I think the Chinese at present are as much of a problem as the Soviet Union, if not more so. I have a feeling that it is not a question of saying the United States shall take the full responsibility—perhaps from an economic point of view, we are the people who can afford it for the time being—perhaps this is an area in which we must make a major contribution. But I do not feel that NATO's only responsibility can be carried out purely by military work; something has to come out of this union of the West in a way of new and fresh approaches to some kind of understanding so that we can live together.

Robert McKenzie. Could we just take a moment to look at feelings here in Britain and Western Europe about the so-called Anglo-American alliance and the present condition of NATO? Because I think it would be unfair if we did not allow American viewers especially, and others as well, to appreciate the degree to which there is uneasiness about certain features of this relationship. I have been recently in Canada, for example, and there was a great deal of apprehension about the fact that on a matter such as the recognition of Communist China, to take an illustration, the American position is so inflexible that the chances of easing tension between East and West seem to be drastically minimized.

Mrs. Roosevelt. But I think you do not realize that that American position is changing. I can take any group in the United States and talk, and put before them the facts that you cannot ever have real disarmament till you have total membership in the United Nations, and get entire agreement from an enormous audience.

Lord Boothby. But, Mrs. Roosevelt, wouldn't you also agree that at the moment NATO is in a terrible mess? There is at present no political direction of NATO at all. You have an invisible strategic committee of ourselves and the United States in Washington; you have an impotent council of second-grade officials in Paris which can do nothing; you have a Supreme Commander taking orders from a vacuum; and you have no coordination, no centralized policy at all; in fact, we are conducting a global war, the West against the forces of communism, without any central organ of political decision.

Mrs. Roosevelt. I couldn't agree with you more, and for some time I have been wondering seriously (this represents a personal opinion, and not a political party's opinion even) whether as it is at the present time, NATO, which had been created to meet certain conditions which no longer exist, does not need serious revision, and whether it could be made what it ought to be—which is a strong group of people thinking alike in the Western part of Europe and with America included, and actually working towards ways to find agreement.

Hugh Gaitskell. This seems to me a wonderful opportunity for us to tell the American people what we would like them to do. I would say, first of all, we would like them to revise their China policy. It is not because we have any illusions about China, but because we believe that the isolation of China is one of the worst things that is happening at the moment. It is this that is partly responsible for the Chinese line on the ideological struggle with Russia, and their belief that war is inevitable. Therefore we think that China should be recognized and brought into the United Nations; and that is pretty universal here. Then I would say, secondly, that we want to see a policy in NATO which does not rely so much upon the use of nuclear weapons. This, I think, is also the view of some American forces, but at the moment the danger is that even quite a small outbreak or attack from the East is to be met by nuclear weapons, and this really will not do. The emphasis must be shifted on to conventional and away from nuclear.

Robert McKenzie. Does that mean that Britain ought to be prepared also to contribute largely conventional forces?

Hugh Gaitskell. I think we should certainly be prepared to go back at least to what we promised we would do some years ago, before divisions in Europe.

Robert McKenzie. Even if it meant restoration of National Service [compulsory military service]?

Hugh Gaitskell. I don't think it would mean that. It can be done, in my opinion, quite easily by increased mobility, by liquidating some of the commitments—which I think are pretty pointless ones—that we have abroad, and by considerably greater efficiency in conventional arms.

Lord Boothby. I think that is an illusion, you know. I do not think that we can carry out our commitments in the field of conventional forces without a restoration of limited National Service, and that sooner or later any British Government will be forced to face up to that.

Increasing the Danger of an Accident

Hugh Gaitskell. Then I think, thirdly, it is enormously important that American policy should be directed against the spread of nuclear weapons within NATO and that is one of the reasons why we also believe we should not have our own.

Mrs. Roosevelt. I could not again, as an individual, agree with you more. Every time we spread the ownership or the possibility of having nuclear weapons we increase the danger of an accident, which is just as dangerous.

Robert McKenzie. I have attended the two American conventions this summer, and it is curious how unaware people making policy in the two parties appear to be of this kind of problem. I was, on the whole, encouraged by the lack of chauvinism and so on, although all kinds of provocations were being delivered by Khrushchev at the same time; but there's a curious blankness when it comes to appreciating the kind of worry you get here in Western Europe about, say, the universal spread of nuclear weapons.

Mrs. Roosevelt. You are entirely right, because we are far removed and we do not understand the feeling. I have just been in Poland; Mr. Gaitskell has just been in Yugoslavia. How many people in our country, except perhaps the little group that came from Poland and Yugoslavia, have the remotest idea of the fears in those two countries?

Lord Boothby. Or that they themselves are in fact in range of Russian missiles at this moment, in the United States? In fact, they do not know that because they do not want to know.

Mrs. Roosevelt. And, of course, the truth of the matter is that actually the people in Europe are far safer from attack from the Soviet Union than we are in the United States. Three years go, Mr. Khrushchev himself gave me a timetable of how long it would take him, if he had nuclear war, to destroy the whole of Europe and then start on the United States. Today I am sure he would reverse his timetable and tell me how long it would take him to destroy the major points that he wished to destroy in the United States. In that case, you in Europe would not have to be destroyed, but you would be slaves.

Hugh Gaitskell. I may be optimistic here, but I do not believe the problem is so much now the imminent danger of war; it is how to achieve peace, how to get away from the stalemate, the cold war, call it what you like. This is the only other point I want to make about our view, anyway, in the Labour party. We do want to see the West taking a much more positive line towards the settlement of outstanding disputes.

Robert McKenzie. I think we ought to bring our minds to bear on the question: granted the failure is in this whole field of disarmament, where as of now do we begin to try to make headway? Lord Russell, apart from any transcendental view of how you eliminate the whole problem, how do you think we should begin with the problem of attempting to make some kind of headway, however small, on disarmament?

Lord Russell. The Government can always put forward disarmament proposals, and hitherto no power has done so sincerely.

Robert McKenzie. How can you be sure of that?

Work for the Neutral Powers

Lord Russell. Because you can see that it is so. In 1955 we had the most frightful shock because the Russians accepted our proposals, so we withdrew them at once. They were only put forward on the assumption that the Russians would reject them, and that is so all the way through. I am not saying this specially of our side; it is true on both sides; and I think one would have to try to get some agreement about disarmament before putting forward a public proposal; and also we should make more use of the neutrals, because at present each side puts forward a proposal and the other side has to object to it: it is part of the rules of the game that there has to be argument. I should try to get some neutral power to make proposals which appear to it to be impartial—India, perhaps—which neither side is proposing and therefore neither side has reasons of prestige for rejecting. I should do this rather quietly and secretly, and get the two sides if possible to agree before there was any publicity; then I think they could jointly put forward such a proposal.

Hugh Gaitskell. Yes—but I think it is only fair to say that the immediate situation has been created by Russia walking out of the ten-power disarmament conference.

Lord Russell. Yes.

Hugh Gaitskell. And one must say that they have been extremely difficult about any kind of negotiation on controls, which naturally the West wants to establish until everything else is agreed, and that won't do. But I agree with Russell: I think that it would be a very good gesture if the West were to propose the presence of both China and India at the disarmament talks. I personally would go back to the ten-power committee. I do not think that eighty powers are going to produce anything at all. On the testing we have made some progress but it ought to be possible there to clear up the few remaining points which divide the two sides; and I think there again you get a small step forward. I would like to see the West also put forward the idea of a zone of controlled disarmament in central Europe because this would give some reassurance to the Poles and the other countries that Mrs. Roosevelt was talking about; initiatives of this kind patiently put forward, expecting a zig-zag policy by the Russians, because we shall certainly have that.

Tackle Political Problems First

Lord Boothby. I am afraid I am in considerable disagreement with both Russell and Gaitskell on this. I am no fan of disarmament conferences, I have seen too many of them fail; and I believe that basically armaments are a symptom of political conditions and therefore that before you get a substantial reduction of armaments you have to solve some of your political problems, and that that should have priority. It is no good talking about disarmament proposals when you have rising political tensions all over the world: tackle the political problems first. One point that Gaitskell made I think is extremely important: a geographical disengagement in Europe would be of immense value. Which brings me right back to where we started—that geographical lines, geographical agreements, are the only ones that the Russians really understand and accept; so I think we ought to work for that.

BIBLIOGRAPHY

An asterisk (*) preceding a reference indicates that the article or a part of it has been reprinted in this book.

BOOKS, PAMPHLETS, AND DOCUMENTS

Banton, M. P. White and coloured; the behavior of British people towards coloured immigrants. Rutgers University Press. New Brunswick, N.J. '60.

Bareau, Paul. Future of the sterling system. Institute of International Affairs. London. '58.

Blackett, P. M. S. Atomic weapons and East-West relations. Cambridge University Press. New York. '56.

Bridges, Sir Edward. Portrait of a profession; the Civil Service tradition. Cambridge University Press. New York. '50.

Brittain, Sir Herbert. British budgetary system. Macmillan. New York. '59.

Bulmer-Thomas, Ivor. Party system in Great Britain. Macmillan. New York. '53.

Burn, Duncan, ed. Structure of British industry; a symposium. 2v. Cambridge University Press. New York. '58.

Butler, D. E. and Rose, Richard. British general election of 1959. St. Martins. New York. '60.

Cardwell, D. S. L. Organisation of science in England. Heinemann. London. '57.

Court, W. H. B. Concise economic history of Britain from 1750 to recent times. Cambridge University Press. New York. '54.

Devlin, Patrick. Trial by jury. Stevens. London. '56.

Economist Intelligence Unit. Britain and Europe. The Unit. 60 East 42d St. New York 17. '58.

Economist Intelligence Unit. Commonwealth and Europe. The Unit. 60 East 42d St. New York 17. '60.

European Free Trade Association. (Published jointly by the governments of Austria, Denmark, Great Britain, Norway, Portugal, Sweden, and Switzerland.) Distributed by British Information Services. 45 Rockefeller Plaza. New York 20. '59.

Flanders, Allan and Clegg, H. A. eds. System of industrial relations in Great Britain; its history, laws, and institutions. Blackwell. London. '54.

Glass, Ruth. Newcomers: the West Indians in London. Allen and Unwin. London. '60.

*Great Britain. British Information Services. Britain and Europe; speech by Selwyn Lloyd before the House of Commons on July 25, 1960. The Services. 45 Rockefeller Plaza. New York 20. '60.

*Great Britain. British Information Services. Britain in brief. The Services. 45 Rockefeller Plaza. New York 20. '59.

Great Britain. British Information Services. British Parliament. The Services. 45 Rockefeller Plaza. New York 20. '59.

Great Britain. British Information Services. Contemporary Britain. The Services. 45 Rockefeller Plaza. New York 20. '59.

*Great Britain. British Information Services. Education in Britain. (Fact Sheets on Britain. R.2541/8.) The Services. 45 Rockefeller Plaza. New York 20. Ap. '58.

Great Britain. British Information Services. Education in Great Britain. The Services. 45 Rockefeller Plaza. New York 20. '58.

Great Britain. British Information Services. Farming Britain. The Services. 45 Rockefeller Plaza. New York 20. '57.

Great Britain. British Information Services. Government and administration of the United Kingdom. The Services. 45 Rockefeller Plaza. New York 20. '60.

*Great Britain. British Information Services. Nuclear energy in Britain. (Fact Sheets on Britain. R.2541/19.) The Services. 45 Rockefeller Plaza. New York 20. Ja. '59.

Great Britain. British Information Services. Queen and people, by Dermot Morrah. The Services. 45 Rockefeller Plaza. New York 20. '60.

Great Britain. British Information Services. Western cooperation in brief. The Services. 45 Rockefeller Plaza. New York 20. '59.

Great Britain. Central Office of Information. Britain, an official handbook.
        Published annually.

Hall, M. P. Social services of modern England. Routledge. London. '59.

Keith, A. B. British Cabinet system. Stevens. London. '52.

Kissinger, H. A. Necessity for choice. Harper. New York. '61.

McKenzie, K. R. English Parliament. Penguin Books. Baltimore. '59.

Morrah, Dermot. Work of the Queen. Kimber. London. '59.

Robbins, A. P. Newspapers today. Oxford. New York. '56.

Thomas, Hugh, ed. The Establishment; a symposium. Potter. New York. '60.

United States. Senate. Western Europe; a study prepared at the request of the Committee on Foreign Relations, by the Foreign Policy Research Institute, University of Pennsylvania. 86th Congress, 1st session. Supt. of Docs. Washington 25, D.C. '59.

PERIODICALS

*Atlantic Monthly. 205:26+. Je. '60. Atlantic report on the world today—London.

Atlantic Monthly. 206:4+. S. '60. Atlantic report on the world today—London.

*British Affairs. 3:7+. Mr. '59. Examinations!

British Affairs. 3:22-6. Je. '59. British electoral procedure.

*British Affairs. 3:194-8. D. '59. Commonwealth.

British Affairs. 4:2-6. Mr. '60. Law. Lord Shawcross.

British Affairs. 4:90-2. Je. '60. Rehousing Britain.

British Affairs. 4:98-101. Je. '60. Social security in Britain. Sir Geoffrey King.

British Affairs. 4:116-21. S. '60. Nuclear power in Britain. Sir Roger Makins.

British Affairs. 4:122-7. S. '60. Britain and the underdeveloped countries. Paul Bareau.

Bulletin of the Atomic Scientists. 15:260-5. Je. '59. British Lords debate nuclear disarmament. M. M. Simpson.

*Bulletin of the Atomic Scientists. 16:123-6. Ap. '60. Non-nuclear club. Ritchie Calder.

Business Week. p 61-2+. Ap. 11, '59. New kind of revolution for Britain.

Commentary. 29:380-6. My. '60. England, the bomb, the marchers. David Marquand.

*Commentary. 30:489-96. D. '60. England's Labor party and its discontents. David Marquand.

Commonweal. 70:419-20. Ag. 14, '59 New class society? M P. Fogarty.

Commonweal. 71:43-5. O. 9, '59. Britain to the polls. M. P. Fogarty.

Commonweal. 71:569-71. F. 19, '60. Morals and medicine. M. P. Fogarty.

Current History. 37:267-71. N. '59. British flexibility and the cold war. G. F. Hudson.

Economist. 196:621-2. Ag. 13, '60; 196:705-6. Ag. 20, '60. Premier and Parliament.

Foreign Affairs. 35:225-37. Ja. '57. Britain and the Common Market. Roy Harrod.

Foreign Affairs. 37:419-31. Ap. '59. Class and conflict in British foreign policy. Peregrine Worsthorne.

Foreign Affairs. 39:81-91. O. '60. Britain's defenses, commitments and capabilities. Michael Howard.

Foreign Affairs. 39:112-22. O. '60. Britain, the Six and American policy. Miriam Camps.

Foreign Policy Bulletin. 39:189-91. S. 1, '60. Britain faces prosperity. R. K. Webb.

Fortune. 62:111-12. O. '60. Britain and the inner Six.

*Harper's Magazine. 213:61-5. N. '56. England gets a race problem. N. I. MacKenzie.

Harper's Magazine. 218:88-91. Mr. '59. Elegant professional who is running England. W. S. White.

*Harper's Magazine. 218:32-7. My. '59. Socialized medicine, ten years old. Don Cook.

Harper's Magazine. 219:31-8. Ag. '59. Mirror for Anglo-Saxons. Martin Green.

Harper's Magazine. 221:52-9. O. '60. Our exiled airmen in England. Clancy Sigal.

*Listener. 113:158-9. Ja. 28, 60. Prime Minister as an elected monarch. R. W. K. Hinton.

    Also reprinted in Parliamentary Affairs, journal of the Hansard Society for Parliamentary Government.

Listener. 114:3-4. Jl. 7, '60. Get in or keep out? Alan Day.

*Listener. 114:207-9. Ag. 11, '60. Irresponsible society. R. M. Titmuss.

*Listener. 114:543-8. O. 6, '60. Prospects of mankind; discussion. Eleanor Roosevelt, Bertrand Russell, Hugh Gaitskell, Lord Boothby, and Robert McKenzie.

Monthly Labor Review. 82:873. Jl. '59. Technical training in the United Kingdom.

Monthly Labor Review. 83:449-59. My. '60; 83:561-8. Je. '60. Housing in Britain and America. D. K. Newman.

*Nation. 188:337-9. Ap. 18, '59. British opinion marches. Norman Birnbaum.

Nation. 189:21. Jl. 18, '59. Contagion of sanity.

New Republic. 140:10-11. Ap. 6, '59. Medical care in Britain. A. T. Moore.

New Republic. 141:7. N. 16, '59. British Africa's future.

New York Times. p 27. S. 9, '58. London weighing migration idea. Drew Middleton.

New York Times. p 3. F. 25, '60. British-American club. Drew Middleton.

*New York Times. p 23. O. 16, '60. British economy reported lagging. W. H. Waggoner.

New York Times. p 12. O. 17, '60. Paradox in Britain. Drew Middleton.

*New York Times. p E7. O. 23, '60. British still hope for 1961 summit. Drew Middleton.

New York Times. p 7. N. 7, '60. Britain and White House. Drew Middleton.

New York Times. p 2. D. 31, '60. Britain and trade unity. Drew Middleton.

New York Times. p 1+. Mr. 16, '61. South Africans decide to leave Commonwealth. W. H. Waggoner.

New York Times. p 3. Mr. 16, '61. Long ties ended by South Africa.

New York Times. p 2. Mr. 17, '61. British grouping based on Empire.

New York Times. p 3. Mr. 17, '61. Britain's problem. Drew Middleton.

New York Times. p 3. Mr. 19, '61. South Africa's future confused without a Commonwealth role. Leonard Ingalls.

New York Times. p 3. Mr. 19, '61. Verwoerd sees new defections. W. H. Waggoner.

New York Times. p 10. Ap. 3, '61. Impassioned marchers; British foes of atomic arms reflect [in fourth annual Aldermaston march] people's ancient tradition of protest. Drew Middleton.

New York Times Magazine. p 24+. My. 17, '59. How Britain makes foreign policy. Drew Middleton.

New York Times Magazine. p 15+. O. 18, '59. Europe goes American—on the surface. Geoffrey Gorer.

New York Times Magazine. p 38+. Ja. 17, '60. In Britain, the U's still have it. Charles Hussey.

New York Times Magazine. p 23+. Mr. 13, '60. Germany: British doubts vs. French logic. Drew Middleton.

New York Times Magazine. p 37+. Mr. 20, '60. Congress or Parliament, which? J. C. Harsch.

*New York Times Magazine. p 12+. Ap. 17, '60. British Tory—far from Tory. Drew Middleton.

New York Times Magazine. p 9+. Je. 14, '60. Britain's Conservatives—and ours. J. C. Harsch.

*New York Times Magazine. p 38-9+. N. 13, '60. Again the timeless flow of ritual. James Morris.

New York Times Magazine. p 24-5+. D. 4, '60. Reflections on the Chatterley case. James Morris.

*New York Times Magazine. p 12+. D. 11, '60. Deeper meaning of British neutralism. Drew Middleton.

Newsweek. 53:38. My. 4, '59. Boiling pots.

Newsweek. 54:103. S. 28, '59. Managed England. Henry Hazlitt.

Newsweek. 54:49-50. O. 26, '59. Winning team.

Newsweek. 55:42. My. 2, '60. I like life: ban the bomb march.

Newsweek. 55:51-2. My. 16, '60. Toward a unified Europe.

Newsweek. 56:32-3. Ag. 8, '60. Shuffle and a sizzle.

Reporter. 20:23-5. Mr. 19, '59. Britain and the bomb. Alistair Buchan.

Reporter. 20:28-31. My. 28, '59. Old order cometh: Britain's new feudalism. C. G. Curran.

Reporter. 20:34-6. Je. 25, '59. On learning and loyalty. J. H. Peck.

*Reporter. 21:13-16. Jl. 9, '59. Britain and Europe at sixes and sevens. Don Cook.

Reporter. 21:22-3. Jl. 23, '59. Britain and the bomb. Peregrine Worsthorne.

Reporter. 23:33-40. S. 29, '60. Decline of the Labour party. George Steiner.

Saturday Evening Post. 233:25+. Jl. 30, '60. Home of the Prime. Don Cook.

*Saturday Review. 42:14-15. O. 17, '59. Are the English being Americanized? Anthony Sampson.

Saturday Review. 43:25. Je. 4, '60. Bridey and the Queen: British television coverage. R. L. Shayon.

Saturday Review. 43:28. Je. 18, '60. Goggle-box. R. L. Shayon.

Science. 129:689-93. Mr. 13, '59. Organization of science in the United Kingdom. E. S. Hiscocks.

Science. 129:952. Ap. 10, '59. Britain's department of industrial and scientific research.

Science. 130:966-7. O. 16, '59. Science enters the political arena.

Science. 130:1099. O. 23, '59. British science attains Cabinet status.

Senior Scholastic. 74:2+. F. 13, '59. New British schools.

Senior Scholastic. 75:12-13. N. 4, '59. Britain: the lion roars again. Eric Berger.

Sunday Times (London). p 10. Jl. 10, '60. Britain must choose soon. Raymond Aron.

*Sunday Times (London). p 10. O. 2; p 10. O. 9; p 10. O. 16; p 10. O. 23, '60. Our affluent society. Aidan Crawley.

Time. 73:25-6. Ap. 20, '59. Strange British mood.

Time. 73:29-30. Je. 8, '59. Status war.

Time. 73:13-19. Je. 29, '59. Redeemed empire.

Time. 73:78+. Je. 29, '59. Buoyant Britain.

*Time. 74:33-6+. O. 19, '59. Art of the practical.

Time. 74:22. O. 26, '59. Aftermath.

Time. 75:36+. Ap. 11, '60. Headlines from the clubroom.

Time. 75:39. Ap. 11, '60. Solidarity of silence.

Time. 75:26. Ap. 25, '60. Scrapping the missiles.

Time. 75:24-5. My. 16, '60. Lengthening shadow: Commonwealth Prime Ministers' conference.

Time. 76:20-2. Ag. 8, '60. House and home.

Time. 76:30+. S. 19, '60. Isles of the blest.

*U.S. News & World Report. 42:100+. Mr. 8, '57. Youths leave Britain.

*U.S. News & World Report. 48:52-3. F. 8, '60. Looking for new role in world—Britain faces major shift.

U.S. News & World Report. 48:95. Ap. 4, '60. Silence strike worries Britain.

U.S. News & World Report. 48:104-5. My. 2, '60. British kitchens are going American.

*U.S. News & World Report. 48:80-1. My. 9, '60. Will the British Commonwealth hold together?

U.S News & World Report 49:74-5 Jl. 8, '60. Where state medicine has had a real tryout.

United States. Department of State Bulletin. 41:405-9. S. 21, '59. Television report by the President and the Prime Minister.

Vogue. 136:102+. S. 15, '60. New Britain. J. H. Listowel.

*Vital Speeches of the Day. 26:290-4. Mr. 1, '60. Commonwealth independence and interdependence; address delivered on February 3, 1960, before both houses of Parliament of the Union of South Africa. Harold Macmillan.